The Abingdon Preaching Annual
2019

The Abingdon
Preaching
Annual

2019

Scott Hoezee, General Editor

 Abingdon Press™

Nashville

THE ABINGDON PREACHING ANNUAL 2019:
PLANNING SERMONS AND SERVICES FOR FIFTY-TWO SUNDAYS

Copyright © 2018 by Abingdon Press

This book is printed on acid-free paper.

Library of Congress Cataloging-in-Publication Data has been requested.

ISBN 978-1-5018-5885-7

Frank A. Thomas. *How to Preach a Dangerous Sermon*, copyright © 2018 by Abingdon Press. Used by permission. All rights reserved.

Kenyatta A. Gilbert. *Exodus Preaching: Crafting Sermons about Justice and Hope*, copyright © 2018 by Abingdon Press. Used by permission. All rights reserved.

Thomas H. Troeger. *The End of Preaching*, copyright © 2018 by Abingdon Press. Used by permission. All rights reserved.

Scripture quotations unless noted otherwise are taken from the Common English Bible, copyright 2011. Used by permission. All rights reserved.

Scripture marked NRSV is from the New Revised Standard Version Bible, copyright © 1989 National Council of the Churches of Christ in the United States of America. Used by permission. All rights reserved worldwide. http://nrsvbibles.org/

18 19 20 21 22 23 24 25 26 27—10 9 8 7 6 5 4 3 2 1
MANUFACTURED IN THE UNITED STATES OF AMERICA

Contents

Contents

🖋 = Sunday in Lent   ☀ = Sunday of Advent

ESSAYS FOR SKILL-BUILDING

FULL SERMON TEXTS

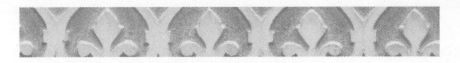

Acknowledgments

This 2019 edition of the *Abingdon Preaching Annual* is now the third such volume for which I have been privileged to serve as general editor. I am grateful to Abingdon for the confidence they placed in me to oversee these projects and am so very grateful to everyone who made this volume as well as the previous two books possible. I am grateful to every person who said yes when in spring 2017 I asked him or her to contribute four or so Sundays' worth of sermon starter reflections and liturgical helps. I have been impressed by each person's creativity and generous spirit. Most, if not all, of the contributors to this volume are themselves busy pastors or professors who had to make time to do the additional work required to be part of this project. I am so thankful they did!

Constance Stella and Peggy Shearon of Abingdon Press/The United Methodist Publishing House were there every step along the way—as were the good people who sent out contracts, looked up copyrights, did page designs, and made sure that all things were done in good order. My son, Graham Apol Hoezee, interned for my office in the summer of 2017 and as part of his work he formatted, edited, and checked scripture citations for the bulk of this book, and I am grateful to him for his work. I am also grateful to my Center for Excellence in Preaching colleague Mary Bardolph, who in both of the previous volumes and now this year's as well helped to make the formatting consistent and developed the book's indices. Mary makes my working life both possible and easier every week, and her help on this book is part and parcel of her excellent work!

—*Scott Hoezee, General Editor*

Editor's Introduction

Although this book is for the calendar year 2019, the bulk of the work on this volume took place across spring, summer, and autumn of 2017. At about the same time I was approaching various pastors and professors to see if they would agree to write for me in the spring of 2017, it was also the fiftieth anniversary of the release of the landmark album *Sgt. Pepper's Lonely Hearts Club Band* by The Beatles. And, of course, a signature song on that album is the one on which Ringo Starr sings lead vocals to declare, "I get by with a little help from my friends."[1] Indeed, we all do.

So think of this 2019 preaching annual as "a little help" from your friends/fellow pastors who took the time to ponder lectionary texts, come up with preaching nuggets and ideas, and compose various litanies, prayers, benedictions, and other liturgical pieces. None of us can do the high and holy task of leading worship and preaching God's word without all the help we can get. The preacher may stand alone in the pulpit every Sunday morning but every preacher knows that right behind him or her stands all those people who wrote commentaries, study aids, and essays to help the preacher bring yet another sermon to life.

Our hope in providing this book is that when a preacher turns to the material for any given Sunday or holy day in 2019, something will leap out, something will trigger a new creative spark, something will give the preacher that one thing that feels fresh and new—even on a Bible text that is otherwise so utterly familiar. If that happens as a result of the writings in this book, then all of us who contributed will be so very grateful that we can see yet again that we really do get by with a little help from our friends.

—*Scott Hoezee, General Editor*

January 6, 2019–Epiphany

Passages: *Isaiah 60:1-6; Psalm 72:1-7, 10-14; Ephesians 3:1-12; Matthew 2:1-12*

Preaching Theme

One of the powerful shaping aspects of the lectionary is that it brings us back to pivotal stories year after year. For instance, the Epiphany texts are always the same, leading us to the magi searching for the newborn king. There is much in their encounter with Jesus that is worth remembering regularly: the fact that their search symbolizes all of our searches for God; that their worshipping presence proves God's grand salvific scope is for all people and not just the Jews; that Herod's response is controlled by fear, like so much of our world; and that the magi's response to a living encounter with the one true God is to worship!

But perhaps the most overlooked truth we encounter in the magi's seeking and finding is how nonchalant and seemingly normal the work of God is in this story. It begins, "After Jesus was born in Bethlehem..." Epiphany is the time to celebrate and recognize that our God "manifests" or "appears" on earth: God is revealed and God's purposes for the world are made known. The magi only have something to seek because Jesus is born God incarnate. The magi only have something to seek because God places in the heavens something to celebrate and reveal Jesus's birthplace. The magi only have something to seek because they are curious to know what is behind the revelation of the star that they understand in part, but not in whole. All of this happens simply because "Jesus was born in Bethlehem." It's as though we are to get the message that God's manifesting is as normal and down-to-earth, as regular and essential to life, as the birth of a baby. By encountering this story over and over, we are invited to find today what the magi found then. God's manifestations may no longer be in the form of a star to mark Jesus's birthplace, but the Holy Spirit continues to reveal God's purposes in the world for those curious enough to investigate the everyday manifestations of God's presence on earth.

Secondary Preaching Themes

Kingship weaves its way throughout the texts for Epiphany. The magi refer to Jesus as the "newborn king." Psalm 72 is a prayer of blessing upon a good king—one who rules with God's judgment and righteousness and whose actions bring peace and justice. This king is a deliverer of the needy, is compassionate on the weak, and redeems the oppressed. Sound familiar? It is essentially the "secret plan" of God made known in Christ Jesus that Paul speaks of in Ephesians 3:1-12. Though Paul does not describe Jesus as king, he does draw the church into the work of "manifesting" the wisdom of Christ the king: "God's purpose is now to show the rulers and powers in the heavens the many different varieties of his wisdom through the church." In other words, as part of the narrative shaped by the lectionary, Psalm 72 becomes a prayer for the church to live out the rule of Christ for all the world to see. Isaiah 60's command to "Arise! Shine!" becomes a call to action in the character of the King of kings. In this way, we become the ordinary appearances of the living God, piquing curiosity of people of every nation, perhaps leading them to an encounter with the living God.

Call to Confession (Based on Ephesians 3:1-12)

The Apostle Paul reminds us that, "In Christ we have bold and confident access to God through faith in him." Even while confessing our sins, we can be confident that it is the forgiving God who listens as we pray. We come with boldness, seeking to be transformed by our repentance. God's purpose throughout all time has been to bring us together with himself; therefore we take the time now to confess what continues to separate us.

Bidding Prayer (Based on Isaiah 60:1-6)

Light of the world, we trust you to make yourself known.
We name the darkness that covers the earth…
We cry out for the gloom that controls the nations…
God in your glory, shine upon them.
For our sons and daughters who are far away…
For those who are not strong enough to stand on their own…
For those whom your light has gathered…
God in your glory, shine upon them.
Like the nations that come with gifts and to proclaim, we offer our praises…
God in your glory, shine upon us.
Amen.

Offering Introduction

The magi brought gifts along with their worship. The psalmist declares that kings will bow down and present gifts to God's good king. We continue this same practice by presenting our monetary gifts to God's kingdom use along with our worship and acts of service.

Sending (Based on Isaiah 60:1-6)

Arise! Shine! Go into the world with confidence that
Our Light has come!
Arise! Shine! Go into the world with confidence that
The Lord will shine upon us!
Arise! Shine! Go into the world with confidence that
God's glory will appear!

January 13, 2019

Passages: Isaiah 43:1-7; Psalm 29; Acts 8:14-17; Luke 3:15-17, 21-22

Call to Worship (Based on Psalm 29)

You, divine beings! Give to the Lord—
We give the Lord glory and power!
Give to the Lord the glory due his name!
We bow down to the Lord in holy splendor!
In his temple everyone shouts,
"Glory!"
The Lord sits enthroned,
He is king forever!

Transition to be used multiple times (based on Psalm 29:9)
In his temple everyone shouts,
"Glory!"

Preaching Theme

Isaiah 43 captures the vocation of our trinitarian God. God the Father is our creator, he formed us and called us by name; Yahweh sees us as precious, he loves us. God the Son redeems us and is the holy one of Israel, our Savior; he is the ransom that has been paid, the one who has taken our place when we were in need of rescuing. We are called by the name of our Savior, Christ, when we are called Christian. God the Holy Spirit is God with us, whose word and breath blows to the corners of the earth, carrying the good news to the far reaches of the earth in order to gather up all of God's sons and daughters. The Holy Spirit is the God who is with us when we pass through the waters and walk through the fire. The Father preserves us through the Spirit's presence in the direst of circumstances.

That such a God would honor us, love us, sacrifice for us, and know us by name! This is the God who fights for what belongs to him. He is present and invested in his handiwork. This is the most intense loving relationship we can imagine. It is one we do not deserve; and yet, this is who our good God has revealed himself to be in word and deed.

Considering that Isaiah 43 was written in the context of exile, what power does such a description of God provide? Though God had not yet revealed himself as triune, God did mean to instill hope in his people, deeply rooted in his character and activity. The people brought their exile upon themselves, but God does not abandon what he has made (or even step away from it as the clock-maker God of deism is depicted). Though their sinfulness and habitual ignoring of the presence of God led them to the troubled waters of exile, God's statements of presence undergird them with the hope that they are not a lost cause, no matter the circumstances. Finally, it firmly reminds God's people that our worth has nothing to do with what we do or do not do, but comes solely from the worth given to us by God because we are God's beloved, created, formed, and made for his glory.

Secondary Preaching Themes

In two of our passages God speaks; in a third, his voice is described in great detail. God's voice is depicted as extremely powerful—enough to shake apart and lay the forest bare. It thunders and unleashes fiery flames, causing the wilderness to shudder at its sound. God's voice is majestic and strong: there is no earthly thing that can withstand its might. Yet, it is with that voice that God speaks blessing and pleasure upon God's beloved. What a comfort to think that the same voice that said to Jesus, "You are my Son, whom I dearly love; in you I find happiness" is the same voice that says to us, "Don't fear, for I have redeemed you; I have called you by name; you are mine. . . . Because you are precious in my eyes, you are honored, and I love you." The power of God's voice assures us of the strength of the promises said in tenderness. It is through these words that God continues to show up to guide and shape what (and who) he has made.

Taken together, our passages sing of the covenant relationship between God and God's people: there's something for everyone to do. God promises protection and provision in Isaiah 43; God's people worship the Lord who gives them strength in Psalm 29. In Luke 3, Jesus joins humanity in being baptized by John the Baptist, even though he had no need for repentance; for his part, John points beyond himself to Jesus by giving to the Lord the glory due him—just as the psalmist encourages. Finally, in some mysterious way, it takes the laying on of hands and the prayers of Peter and John to call down the Holy Spirit in Samaria. God is so invested in his creation that he engages creatures in the continuation and spread of his glory.

Prayer for Illumination

As we hear your word, may we hear your strong and majestic voice. May we trust your words of promise and presence. Amen.

Benediction (Based on Isaiah 43:1-7)

God preserve you through the rising waters and fires of life.
God call you by name and gather you when you drift away.
Because you are precious in his eyes.
God loves you.

January 20, 2019

Passages: Isaiah 62:1-5; Psalm 36:5-10; 1 Corinthians 12:1-11; John 2:1-11

Call to Worship (Based on Psalm 36:5-10)
We come to the house of the Lord to drink from the spring of life. Let us see in his light today.

Preaching Theme

Imagine reaching the places depicted by Psalm 36. What does it take to get to the skies or to reach the clouds? Flight for humans only comes in a few forms, and there are more of us who have never felt the air on our skins at 12,500 feet above ground level (the standard altitude for skydiving) than those who have. Similarly, very few of us have scaled up the sides of the sturdiest rock formations and mountains in the world. To reach the top of the strongest mountains takes elite training and resources and a whole lot of time. And like the skies above, but even more extreme, no one can place their feet on the deepest depths of the ocean and live to tell the tale. James Cameron has been there in a submarine, and his words for describing how it felt: desolation and isolation.[1]

To get to all of these places, human beings have to work really hard, spend a lot of time and resources to do it, and even then, we fail to get the full experience they have to offer because our bodies simply cannot handle them. Yet, God's loyal love has no problem extending to the skies. Yahweh's faithfulness draws our eyes up past the clouds looking for its end. God's righteousness, the measure of holiness, cannot be scaled by our own strength, and we will give up on trying to do it because there will be obstacles that are impassable to us. The justice of our God runs so deep that no human could survive being there! Our presence in each of these places is always mediated in some way—equipment, vessels, training programs meant to protect and prepare us. What an apt reminder of the work of Christ on the cross on our behalf, our true mediator to the work of God.

Secondary Preaching Themes

Jesus's first miracle in the Gospel of John takes place at a wedding feast as he supplies the wine for the celebration when the groom's runs out. This matrimonial backdrop pairs well with both Isaiah 62 and Psalm 36, where love and marriage come into even sharper focus. Jesus supplies wine for guests at a wedding, but in all actuality, he is the spring of life, and we drink from his river of joy—these will never be under threat of running out like the party wine. Psalm 36 describes God as having loyal love, a faithful love that is priceless. These are the things we hope for at weddings, but cannot guarantee. And in both the "marriages" of Isaiah 62 and John 2, someone else shines because of what God does. Jesus doesn't take the credit for the wine, but allows the headwaiter to praise the groom; in Isaiah, God promises to make his bride, Jerusalem, shine out like a light.

One easily gets the sense from these texts that our God is a generous God. Yahweh saves people and animals; he calls us by new names and reverses not only our personal fortunes, but the land's as well. God's love, faithfulness, righteousness, and justice are so large that the earth cannot contain them. Jesus provides the libations at a party! And the Holy Spirit gives its many gifts to each of us in different ways, which, when woven together, blesses the world. From the spiritual to the physical, God is generous with his love, his power, and even himself.

Prayer (Based on 1 Corinthians 12:1-11)

We thank you, Holy Spirit, for giving and demonstrating yourself through us. We thank and praise you for your activity today. Manifest your presence among us and encourage us to share for the good of the church.
For the gifts of wisdom and words of knowledge to direct us in hard times,
Thanks be to God.
For the gift of faith that continuously points us to Christ at all times,
Thanks be to God.
For the gifts of healing and miracles that proclaim your real presence in painful times,
Thanks be to God.
For the gifts of prophecy and discernment to help us find you in murky times,
Thanks be to God.
And for the gifts of speaking and interpreting in what otherwise might be confusing times,
Thanks be to God.

Prayer for Illumination (Based on Psalm 36:5-10)

Hearing your word in community, we find ourselves feasting on the bounty of your house, drinking from your river of pure joy. For you, God, are the spring of our lives. In the reading of scripture, may we see your light. May you make our hearts right by your transforming power. Amen.

Benediction (Based on Isaiah 62:1-5)

May the God who delights in you make you shine with the holiness of Christ. May God rejoice because of you and call you by his new name for you, beloved.

"On Being Jesus's Mother"

John 2:1-11

Karoline M. Lewis

We know her as Mary. But Jesus's mother in the Gospel of John is not the Mary we thought we knew. She's never called Mary, only the mother of Jesus. And of course in John, there's no traditional birth narrative—no stable and shepherds and angels. No harrowing birth story of having a baby in a most unexpected place. No visitors to the hospital from the east. No gifts of congratulations.

Just a cosmic birth story with the Word becoming flesh—and in that version of Jesus's birth, no mention of Jesus's mother, at all.

She appears only twice in John's story—at the wedding at Cana and at the foot of the cross. She's there for Jesus's first sign and then hears him let out his last breath. At the beginning of his ministry and at its end. She brackets the incarnation, if you will. And she is the first one in the Gospel of John to show us what discipleship looks like.

I think a lot of times we make discipleship rather complicated. Or get all caught up in rules we should be following when we don't really do a good job of that anyway. The mother of Jesus teaches us that sometimes all God needs us to do is to be. To be present. To abide.

It's her abiding, her presence, that gets Jesus's ministry going.

Have you ever noticed that in the Gospel of John?

She's the one who pushes Jesus out the door.

She's the one who says, "Come on, you can do this, I know who you are. I've seen what you can do." After all, there's thirty years of mothering behind what happens at that wedding at Cana.

In John, there's no voice from the heavens saying to Jesus, or anyone else for that matter, "This is my beloved Son, with whom I am well pleased."

In John, there's no temptation in the wilderness for Jesus then to say, "Okay, if I can make it through that, I can make it through anything. I guess I am really God's Son! Let's get this started!"

In John, there's no transfiguration to confirm the claims from heaven stated at Jesus's baptism.

There's just Jesus's mother. She's the initiator, the impetus, the instigator who gets things going. Because sometimes the only thing you need is your mom.

You remember how the story goes. The wedding celebration being attended by Jesus and his mother and the disciples has run out of wine. Not a good thing at a wedding, back then, and now.

But the mother of Jesus knows what needs to be done and what her son can do. "They've run out of wine, Jesus." And Jesus's answer? A paraphrase might be, "Yeah, well, so what, Mom? They should have hired a better wedding planner."

Have you ever wondered what took place between verses 4 and 5? I imagine the conversation going something like this: "Don't give me that, Jesus. It's time, all right. No more renting a room from me and your dad. No more living in the basement. No more excuses or emptying out my refrigerator every time you have friends over. No more endless supply of pizza and pop. No more messing around with this Messiah complex. Oh no, Jesus. Now is the time. You maybe don't see it, but I do. I know who you are."

She knew it was time. It had to be time. Because the world would never be fully ready for what was about to happen. Because the world would never be ready for God becoming human. In fact, the world would reject such an idea for all its worth.

So, the mother of Jesus goes to the steward and says, "Do whatever he tells you."

And to Jesus, she is saying, "Come on, you can do it. I know you can." Like getting your kindergartner to climb on to the school bus for the first time. "Come on, you can do it, get on the bus!"

But to us and everyone else in the story the mother of Jesus says, "If you do what Jesus tells you? Grace upon grace will follow." And so the man ill for thirty-eight years, all of his life to be exact, picks up his mat when Jesus tells him to and walks. The man who had been blind since birth goes to wash in the pool of Siloam when Jesus tells him to, and ends up being one of Jesus's sheep. Lazarus, dead for four days, really, really dead, walks out of the tomb when Jesus tells him to and is then next found reclining on Jesus during dinner. Grace upon grace. All of it.

And it's Jesus's mother who tells Jesus who he is.

This is not a moment for just *any* sign. This is Jesus's first act out of the gate. Not an exorcism. Not a sermon on a mount. Not even a sermon in his hometown of Nazareth. No, it had to be an act of grace upon grace, an act of abundance, six jars, twenty to thirty gallons, filled to the brim, of the best wine, when you least expect it.

The mother of Jesus pushes Jesus into revealing who he is—God's grace upon grace—here and now, right in front of us, among us, abiding with us.

She pushes God into remembering who God decided to be.

I wonder if God needed to be reminded of what God got into.

I mean, God, what were you thinking? Good idea in theory, you wanting to dwell among us, to move into the neighborhood. Sure, you had done that before. We remember those wilderness wandering of days gone by. But you becoming flesh? You becoming us? You becoming human? Well, that's a whole different kind of dwelling. That ups the ante considerably.

No wonder you might have needed a push.

And so God trusts Jesus's mother to be the parent when God cannot be. God is willing to share this parenthood thing. In fact, God has to. Becoming human depends on it. God can't just swoop in for a parenting save. Once you go down the road that is being human it's not like you can change your mind. It's not like you can call a time-out. Kind of like when you decide to be a parent. There's no going back. No, God needs the mother of Jesus to be the parent of God's human self. God needs the mother of Jesus to parent God.

Really, you say? You are talking about God, you know. Really, I say. I know I am talking about God. Our God who became one of us. There's no partially being human, friends. You are either human or you are not.

God needs the mother of Jesus to say to him, "You have to show the world who you are" as God enters the world. And then, God will need her to say, "See? Look what you showed the world" as God leaves the world.

But not only does the mother of Jesus help God see who God decided to be, the mother of Jesus helps us see who God calls us to be, who God needs us to be.

Think about it.

She's watched Jesus.

She knows him.

She's witnessed what he could do.

She sees Jesus for who he is.

And then she says, you can do this. Let me tell you who you are.

It's time for you to be who you are—in the world, for the sake of the world.

Isn't this what we need for ourselves? Who is the mother of Jesus in your life? Who helps you see who God sees you to be? Who affirms who you are, who God has called you to be? Who tells you when they see pieces of you slipping away? And who needs you to be the mother of Jesus for them? That abiding presence. Abiding when really, that's all we have the strength to do.

We know, we see, we have witnessed what they are capable of. And we nudge, we push, and say, "Come on, you can do this." We walk alongside them so that they can walk into the future people God has called them to be.

It seems that Jesus learned a few things from his mother, because isn't this exactly what he does with his disciples? "Friends, you will do greater things than these." And again, "Beloved, as my Father sent me into this world, now I send you." And again, "Peter, *you* are the shepherd now. Feed my sheep."

If Jesus needed to be told who he was, if Jesus needed to be reminded of who he was, how much more so do we?

Discipleship as a call to abiding is taking on the role of the mother of Jesus for someone who needs to be who God needs them to be.

To point out when the jugs are empty.

To say, come and see who you can be.

To help them see who God sees they are.

The mother of Jesus models an essential element of discipleship. One easily overlooked and taken for granted and assumed. Kind of like mothers in general. It's discipleship that acts out assurance, that knows the simple power of presence.

But, don't misunderstand. I am not talking about mere empowerment. This is not pep-talk discipleship. This is not cheering-on-the-sidelines discipleship. This is not coach, trainer, maximizing-your-potential-personal-power or having-your-best-life-now kind of discipleship.

The mother of Jesus does not model a discipleship of encouragement but a discipleship of courage.

Because it takes an awful lot of courage to push your child out the door. And takes even more courage to abide at the foot of a cross and watch your child die.

Sometimes in this world, all we can do is abide. And to abide is sometimes all God needs us to do. Amen.

January 27, 2019

Passages: Nehemiah 8:1-3, 5-6, 8-10; Psalm 19; 1 Corinthians 12:12-31a; Luke 4:14-21

Preaching Theme

When the people gather to hear the word of God, they have already strengthened their faith muscles. Those who were left behind at the exile have followed a man who convinced them they were capable of rebuilding a destroyed city. Thousands of families have returned to their ancestral homes, returning from the security they had learned in Babylon for the unknown of a rebuilt Jerusalem. In other words, the time was ripe for the Spirit's renewal as the people were committed to whatever (or wherever) God had brought them. "Everyone listened attentively to the Instruction scroll" standing outdoors in a large crowd throughout the day as Ezra read. Their response is myriad. Upon hearing the word of the Lord, witnessing Ezra bless "the Lord, the great God…all of the people answered, 'Amen! Amen!' while raising their hands." Then they fell to their knees and put their faces to the ground, moving from standing in respect to the word to reverence for it by humbling themselves before God in worship.

They weep at what they hear. It's not made clear just exactly what their mourning is about, but we can venture to guess based on our own experience of receiving profound truths with a willing and open heart.… In other words, the time was ripe for the rebuilt and repopulated city of God because it was ripe within the hearts and minds of the people gathered there. Perhaps they finally understood that what they contributed to Jerusalem's restoration was good, but what God was doing was greater still—faith had gotten them this far, but God would finish the good work of his will. God invites them to celebrate and to feast, to fuel up, because their faith—our faith—is made resilient by his nourishment.

Secondary Preaching Themes

Three of the texts center on the hearing of and response to God's word. In Nehemiah, it brings the people to tears to hear God's instructions again. The psalmist provides a litany of the benefits of God's instruction. In Luke, Jesus stands up in the synagogue and reads from the prophet Isaiah, proclaiming that he was the fulfillment of scripture. The response of the people in the Old Testament passages points clearly to transformation—the people cry because they are convicted of the way of the Lord, but God's religious leaders tell them this is reason to celebrate! Knowing more of God's ways is a good thing! They can now be changed in all of the ways that the psalmist describes. Yet, our New Testament passage stays silent about the response of those who heard the word of the Lord in that synagogue from Jesus. Will they enter into the celebration and be transformed by the Spirit at work in the word? Many commentators argue that their response would have been neither tears nor submission, but anger. Such anger will shut them out of both the feasting on the word and the revival of their very being. May it not be so with us.

Notice, too, the communal nature of the life of faith. In Nehemiah, the community is gathered to hear the word, with special attention paid that there were people present who would be able to help the people understand what they heard. Psalm 19 is a universal poem that applies to everyone. Jesus speaks and reads while at synagogue: the gathering of the Jewish faith community for instruction. Finally, Paul tells us that God intentionally formed us as a community of faith into a body where no part is expendable, marking the plural shaping of our faith as unquestionable.

Prayer for Illumination (Based on Nehemiah 8:1-3, 5-6, 8-10)

Lord God, we are gathered here to listen attentively to your word. Help us understand what we hear so that the joy of the Lord may be our strength. We bless the Lord, our great God. Amen! Amen!

Responsive Reading/Confession (Based on Psalm 19)

The Lord's instruction is perfect,
It revives our very being.
The Lord's laws are faithful,
They make us wise.
The Lord's regulations are right,
They gladden our hearts.
The Lord's commands are pure,
They give light to our eyes.
Hear the perfect law of God...
(read a summary of the Law or Ten Commandments)

There is great reward in keeping these,
We are enlightened by them.
Yet we cannot know all that we have done wrong, so we pray
May God clear us of any unknown sin and save us from our willful ones.
May God make us blameless and innocent before him.
Amen.

Transition to Congregational Prayer (Based on 1 Corinthians 12:12-31a)

God has gathered us here as his body of believers in such a way that we live and love and become a true family. God's spirit unites us in such a way that when one suffers, we all suffer; when one celebrates, we all celebrate. Therefore, we lift up both the joys and the concerns of our church family in communal prayer.

February 3, 2019

*Passages: Jeremiah 1:4-10; Psalm 71:1-6; 1 Corinthians 13:1-13;
Luke 4:21-30*

Call to Worship

Some Pharisees wanted to test Jesus. So they asked him if it was right for a man to di-
vorce his wife. They said, "Moses allows a man to divorce his wife and send her away."
We will send no one away.
Some people brought their children to Jesus so he could bless them. But his disciples
told the people to stop bothering Jesus.
We will send no one away.
A crowd gathered but had nothing to eat. Jesus called his disciples, saying, "If I send
them fasting to their home, they will faint away, for some of them have come a long
way."
We will send no one away.
We are called into community with one another regardless of our many differences.
We are called to love those who have felt unwelcome in our spaces: those who have
struggled with the acceptance of their identities in religious spaces and those who
have questioned their status as children of God because of our failure to represent
God's love.
**We as a community of faith value diversity and celebrate differences as inten-
tional acts of God's creation. God's love includes all persons, so we welcome and
include all persons regardless of the differences between us. We will send no one
away!**

Preaching Theme

The liturgical theme of Epiphany serves as a backdrop for contemporary con-
templation of this text. Jesus, a familiar person in the community, exhibits an unexpected and emergent prophetic personality that is highlighted with a casual and
sarcastic reference, "Joseph's boy." This can be taken as mere curiosity or amazement
or interpreted as critique. Either deduction brings into question whether a child of
Joseph could be prophetic or prominent in status. This represents not only a self-dep-
recating cultural and communal reflection, but is also a devaluing of the inalienable

rightness and authority that Jesus embodied and sought to endow in those he is purposed to minister and save.

Though forecast centuries before in Isaiah 61, both Jesus's presence and proclamation evidences truth in real time. Epiphany—divine manifestation—is the visual, tangible actualization of otherworldly assurance as acknowledged and experienced in our time.

Not unlike today, people of antiquity suffered under the false misapprehension that Jesus was defined by sociopolitical or genealogical constructs. Jesus is not defined by his connection to this community or lineage. Luke clearly and consistently refers to Jesus as the Son of God. This reality anchors Jesus in kinship with God while forever attaching all of humanity to that shared lineage and legacy. Jesus affirms that God's blessing is not only for an "us." God's grace is not limited by biology, history, or community barriers; it is available to all.

Relationship with God is personal, yet fully realized in community. Thus, it is troublesome when persons see and practice their faith in a vacuum. In order to live our faith, we must be ready to transcend the boundaries that our communities and, too often, our churches have reinforced with radical love and connection.

Secondary Preaching Themes

There is a divine directive presented in 1 Corinthians 13. A Christ-inspired charge to all who profess God through Jesus Christ as Lord and Savior. "Love the Lord your God with all your heart and with all your soul and with all your entire mind. And love your neighbor as yourself." God and God's word expect nothing less from us than love. Anything and everything void of love is nothing.

Paul labors to explain the right and righteous way to exercise all spiritual gifts— the way of love. Paul does not identify love as a gift; rather it is a fruit of the Spirit. Love is the evidence that you are truly gifted and grafted in God through Jesus Christ.

Even the most spectacular manifestations from our gifts mean nothing unless motivated by love. Graciousness in speech and generosity extended in God's name are meaningless if love is absent. Our genius, goals, and great accomplishments are inconsequential if not exercised or anchored in love.

Love never fails because it is not sourced from this world. Verse 8 reads, "Love never fails. As for prophecies, they will be brought to an end. As for tongues, they will stop. As for knowledge, it will be brought to an end." This is so, because such things are partial in nature. It is all finite. It is all temporal and inevitably unnecessary when all is said and done. Divinely sourced love, however, endures.

Benediction

God in whose image we are made
Jesus Christ, the Son, who is our advocate and affirmation
Holy Spirit whose acts lead toward righteousness
Be all power and glory in our lives
Hence now and forever more, Amen

February 10, 2019

*Passages: Isaiah 6:1-8, (9-13); Psalm 138; 1 Corinthians 15:1-11;
Luke 5:1-11*

Call to Worship

We are here, Lord. Now what?
Follow me!
We have dedicated our lives to study, Lord. Now what?
Follow me!
But, we have partners, families, and responsibilities, Lord.
Follow me!
The days of our lives are filled with hurriedness and important task, Lord.
Follow me!
There are bills to pay, obligations to honor, aspirations to fulfill, Lord.
Follow me!
I want to serve you, love your people, and glory your name, but really know how, Lord.
Follow me!
Can't it wait?
Follow me!
Where? For how long?
Follow me!

Preaching Theme

Luke presents the experience of ordinary persons being encountered by an extra-terrestrial agency, for in that moment, this agency forever transforms their life work. Epiphany. It is a story of call.

The fishermen did not do anything meriting such an invitation to enlist into service with Jesus. Neither did they realize the unique skills or depth of understanding they exhibited that were useful to such responsibility. Like in the case of the fishermen, "calling" oft-times is not predicated on familiarity or expertise. In fact, on paper these individuals would have not been considered qualified applicants. Most of these candidates were persons who possessed characters that were in question and skills that were lowly. Yet, God's call is unpredictable, and is always unmerited.

This text also teaches us that our call can avail itself at unexpected times and in unexpected places. The call narrative of the fishermen, as the text illustrates, comes not on a mountaintop or "holy" space, rather in the midst of the mundane, daily work of their vocation. God always shows up for us and to us in the right place and the right time. God's voice may come in a booming voice or a still, small whisper.

Jesus's invitation is not just to "follow me," but instead commissions the disciples to service. Inherent in their respective call is the responsibility of exampling for others, just as Jesus has called and shared in exercise with them. Ultimately, Jesus's call is for a reordering of commitments and purposes to align with word, witness, and worship to God's end. Call is antagonistic toward and antithetical to one's own plans, yet always aligns with God's will and is akin to God's promises. The fishermen must abandon their professional success of their day in favor of their divine call to serve first, not their financial commitments and obligations, but their divine imperative to serve and call others, just as they have been called by Jesus.

Secondary Preaching Themes

Typically, in theater productions, an encore is a sign of immense appreciation for an exceptional performance. The gesture signals the desire for the experience to continue—the audience does not want the performance to end. Audience members clap as they wait for the performers to reappear on the stage for an additional set. Those faithful to Christ should both expect and seek out the reappearing or evidencing of God through Jesus Christ in their lives.

In the Corinthian text, Paul unfolds the dimensions of Christ's series of divine manifestations. Christ shows forth in the message of good news and hope that is alive then and now. Christ is visible, not unlike other postresurrection appearances, in the practice of witness. The faithful of Christ are revisited in Jesus coming alive through us and through our worship and witness.

In verse 9, we once again see that God's call comes to unexpected people in unexpected places. After listing the followers visited by the resurrected Jesus, Paul admits that he is the most unlikely and unworthy to be called by the resurrected Jesus. God's grace and call extend even to Paul, who has been an enemy to the church. Paul's call serves as a model for reflection on our own response to the reappearance of Christ in our daily lives.

Benediction

Now unto God who is our word
Jesus, the Son, who is our witness
Holy Spirit, which is our worship
Carry us forth into the world as a celebration unto YOU with our lives. Amen.

February 17, 2019

Passages: Jeremiah 17:5-10; Psalm 1; 1 Corinthians 15:12-20; Luke 6:17-26

Call to Worship

Blessed are the poor
It is me, Lord
Blessed are the hungry
It is me, Lord
Blessed are those that weep
It is us, Lord
Blessed people who are hated, excluded, and reviled
Our lives matter, Lord
Blessed are those who belong to God
We all belong to you, O Lord. We are blessed!

Preaching Theme

This is a challenging text for many to interpret. Luke's text (commonly referred to as the Beatitudes) points to the manifestation of God in and across our lived experiences. It is challenging because it requires us to see God in places and in ways that are antithetical to the world's priorities and perspectives. As Christians, we are called to use a formula inverse to that provided by society. The world only sees blessing in the signs and wonders that are principally material in nature, ornate by design, signified by status, and socially accepted or approved.

However, God's priorities do not align with the world. God's blessing is grace. It is operating and living in the preferences and expectations of God. God blesses those whom society marginalizes. As James Cone teaches, "Christian theology is a theology of liberation, and its task should be concerned with explicating the meaning of God's liberating activity so that those who labor under enslaving powers will see that forces of liberation are the very activity of God."[1] God is God of the oppressed. God through Jesus Christ intends to liberate the captive; heal the sick; empower the poor and weak; uplift the downtrodden; and radically transform the political, social, and economic systems of this life.

God can and will show up in real and necessary ways. Christians ought to see God evidenced, or made real, in tangible and intangible forms within our lives. Ultimately, if we follow God's call, we will create conflict with the world around us. Society seeks to reinforce its own values, and the prioritizing of God's values will make us antithetical and antagonistic to the world. But through God's grace, we are blessed even in our discomfort. We are blessed through entering into a new way of being in which we reject the rubric that society attempts to use to measure our lives.

Secondary Preaching Theme

To live righteously is to simply live in right alignment with God and God's plan. If your car's wheels are misaligned, it can cause major problems for other parts of the car like the brakes or the wheel bearings. This imbalance of incongruence can adversely affect the car's rate of speed, braking capacity, and gas mileage. This is likewise true in our spiritual lives. We are slow in getting where we are destined to go because we are not properly aligned. We are not maximizing our time, talent, and treasure for the glory of God.

In order to resolve that we will be blessed, there are people we need to avoid. The text points out three specific types of persons and personalities to avoid at all cost in order to be blessed of God and live in righteousness. God's word says that blessed people avoid those who are ungodly. That is to say, persons and personalities who lack moral and ethical integrity. It says to avoid those who are sinners—those professional, habitual wrongdoers who major in mess, mayhem, and manure. God will bless the obedient and the faithful, so we must avoid those who serve as stumbling blocks to us.

Secondly, if you are resolved to be blessed, then there are some priorities you need to establish. Verse 2 tells us that a person who is blessed is so because God centers their joy and desires on the things and ways as prescribed and dictated by God—that is what aligns with the word of God. If you make God your priorities, then your priorities will become God's priorities. If you desire the Lord, you will be blessed!

Finally, you must be planted. Planted, meaning firmly positioned, settled, and established. We must be planted in order to grow! We must reflect on where we are planted and who planted us there. If where you're planted is distanced from God, the things of God, and the people of God, then you need to reflect on where you are planted, because you are possibly planted in some unfertile place with decaying and demonic people. We must rather be planted in God's word and work through our worship to and relationship with God.

Don't wait until tomorrow to begin to rejoice, praise, and celebrate. Resolve to be blessed now and forevermore.

Benediction

Prayer of St. Francis

Lord, make me an instrument of your peace. Where there is hatred, let me sow love; where there is injury, pardon; where there is doubt, faith; where there is despair, hope; where there is darkness, light; where there is sadness, joy.

O, divine master, grant that I may not so much seek to be consoled as to console; to be understood as to understand; to be loved as to love. For it is in giving that we receive; it is in pardoning that we are pardoned; it is in dying that we are born again to eternal life.

February 24, 2019

Passages: Genesis 45:3-11, 15; Psalm 37:1-11, 39-40; 1 Corinthians 15:35-38, 42-50, Luke 6:27-28

Call to Worship

"It is our duty to fight for our freedom.
It is our duty to win.
We must love each other and support each other.
We have nothing to lose but our chains."[2]

Preaching Theme

The Lukan text in chapter 6 reminds believers that our faith is an act of resistance. In a time wrought with indifference and when we are divided across numerous social constructs of inhumane historical precedent, practicing unconditional respect and uplift of others is challenging. Verse 27 of Jesus's sermon transitions from the assurance of blessings to responsibility, to siding with the poor, to the divine imperative of loving enemies. This instructional discourse grounds the Christian ethos. In this text, Jesus is detailing the ways in which God's priorities, which are antithetical to the ways of the world, should shape our actions.

The purpose of Jesus's directions for relinquishing material goods or to practice civil disobedience is to challenge systems, that is to say, Empire. The world's systems, laws, and processes are inherently inhumane and absent of love. Those called of Christ are required to embody and exercise love upon all creation. The narrative notes that love is shown in sacrifice of our stuff and ourselves. This text provides us with a new way of being in relationship with one another. Jesus calls us to respond to others according to God's love. This means that we must abandon our urge to "get even" in order to respond in a way that shares God's love and protects our humanity. When Jesus suggests turning the other cheek after being slapped previously, he is not simply challenging antiquity's "shaming" culture, but encouraging an early exhibition of civil disobedience in the face of dehumanization.

These actions are representations and expressions of truth in the face of power. Jesus's teachings, like all kingdom pathos, are antithetical to the world's assumptions and norms. Democratic, legislative, and social ideals grant allowance for equal or greater response to hurt, harm, or danger if upon an individual or that which they control. When someone mistreats another, it is neither unusual nor unacceptable, across cultures and spaces, to reciprocate such mistreatment. Rather, Christians are called to work in the example of our ultimate ethical witness—Jesus Christ—showing compassion as did the progenitor.

Secondary Preaching Themes

A hallmark of Wesleyan practice is adherence to doing no harm, doing good, and loving God faithfully. The acrostic poetry of Psalm 37 gives credence to such basic instruction. The psalmist reminds believers not to get upset over the wrong in the world. We live in a world that is defined by competition. We are constantly compared to others, and often we internalize this behavior and begin to measure ourselves in relation to others. We ask why bad people receive good things while we continue to struggle. At times, it is easy to look at others and become angry. Harboring anger and rage serves to be unhealthy; those in relationship with the Lord release themselves and others of such. They are admonished to do so knowing that the wrong, evil, and ungodly will not last always.

Even in our struggle, God shows Godself to be present, powerful, and purposeful. The help of the Lord can come in many ways and forms. Verses 39 and 40 remind us that God is our refuge in the face of uncertainty and wickedness. We must reside in God's love, allowing it to transform us even in our moments of anger and resentment. While we may never understand why bad things happen to good people, or why it sometimes seems like the wicked are rewarded, God's love and presence in our life endures. We are comforted knowing that God is always with us, even when we are lost in struggle and confusion.

Benediction

Unto the God whom we trust
The Son whose example of goodness and love we follow
And to the Holy Spirit who shapes, strengthens, and sustains us:
Send us forth into this world in love
Looking onward and upward . . . living to live again!

March 3, 2019–
Transfiguration Sunday

Passages: Exodus 34:29-35; Psalm 99; 2 Corinthians 3:12-4:2;
Luke 9:28-36, (37-43)

Gathering Prayer

Holy God, you call us today to the mountaintop to witness your glory and power. Your faithful love shines upon us, as it did upon Moses, Elijah, and spiritual ancestors before us. Prepare us for surrender and obedience, that we might follow Jesus's example into the sobering journey ahead. Amen.

Preaching Theme

The story of the transfiguration of Jesus is the halfway point of the Gospel. The stories before it introduce Jesus to the world and chronicle the rise of Jesus's popularity through his healing miracles and compelling teaching. After the transfiguration, Jesus turns toward Jerusalem, and toward the passion of Holy Week.

Transfiguration Sunday is therefore the critical pivot of the liturgical year. It transitions the church away from the wonder of Advent and bright hope of Epiphany into the sober, introspective journey through Lent. This mountaintop story is indeed a pinnacle moment, and our descent from this story immerses us more deeply into the call to obedience and surrender.

On many levels, the transfiguration is an intermission between two distinct acts of our spiritual journey. The first act is about getting to know Jesus, and the second is about following Jesus. The preacher may wish to develop this theme more fully, asking the question, "Are you a 'first act' or a 'second act' Christian?"

If the "first act" is about getting to know Jesus, the "second act" is about living his example, allowing Jesus to shape the way we live. If the "first act" of our faith is learning to call ourselves a Christian, then the "second act" of our faith is found in making Christlike sacrifices. If the "first act" of our faith journey is about becoming a mere church supporter, then the "second act" is about allowing Jesus to shape every aspect of our lives. If the "first act" of your faith journey is about getting acquainted with this Jesus, the "second act" is about making him your Lord.

Secondary Preaching Theme

Both Exodus and 2 Corinthians reference the veil that Moses wore as he descended from the mountain. His encounter with God had rendered his face so bright that others were unable to look at him directly. Yet, there are slight differences in the symbolism they ascribe to that veil. In Exodus, the veil is a symbol of protection, as Moses uses the veil to shield onlookers from fully gazing at his face. It is a visible reminder that humans are too finite to comprehend the full glory of God. It is therefore a veil of grace, a means through which people could encounter the fullness of God in more finite, understandable ways.

In 2 Corinthians, Paul does not interpret the veil to be a means of protection for the viewer, but a symbol of one's willful ignorance and rejection of God. It is a sign for a "hardened" heart that renders a person unable to experience God's goodness and love because of one's own wayward choices. There is certainly more indictment and conviction in this interpretation of the veil.

The preacher may wish to hold the Exodus and 2 Corinthians texts in creative tension, asking the question, "Which kind of veil is at work in your life?" Is it a veil of grace, a gift from God that enables you to begin to understand the mysteries and depth of God's work in your life? Or is it a self-imposed veil of willful ignorance that is preventing you from growing in your faith and following Jesus? Or to some degree, is it both?

This is an important question to ponder as the church enters the season of Lent. It is a time to recognize both kinds of veils at work in our spiritual journey. Lent calls us to acknowledge our own finite capacity to comprehend God's love, and remove any pride or self-reliance that would convince us that we are self-sufficient enough to make it through life. But it also calls us to confession, to acknowledge all the ways that we have impeded the free flow of God's grace in our lives.

Prayer Application

God, in the transfiguration of Jesus you revealed the brightness of your love for the world. You have always been at work throughout the history of your people, and your grace has been operating within us before we were even aware of it. May this day bring to us new understanding and new courage to remove the veils of our own ignorance.

We confess to you our disobedience of your will. We are prone to pride and false notions of self-reliance. We far too often choose the way of harm instead of forgiveness, and self-assuredness instead of surrender. As we move through this season of Lent, shine your love once again upon us, that we may follow you along the way that leads to the cross. Amen.

Benediction

Now may the God who meets you on the mountaintop lead you into the valleys of life. May you see the brightness of Christ's love and reflect it for others. And may you be strengthened daily by the Holy Spirit for the journey ahead. Amen.

March 10, 2019– First Sunday in Lent

Passages: Deuteronomy 26:1-11; Psalm 91:1-2, 9-16; Romans 10:8b-13; Luke 4:1-13

Gathering Prayer

God, in Jesus you identified with the sufferings of the world and understand the temptations we face. Call us to greater awareness of your love, that by your Spirit we might overcome all that tempts us. Amen.

Preaching Theme

There is an important principle that connects all three temptations of Jesus, and offers us guidance for how to overcome that which tempts us in our own lives.

First, Jesus was tempted to take some ordinary stones and turn them to bread. He could have done so. He could turn water into wine, after all, and no one would have faulted him for feeding himself when he was hungry. But rather than use the full powers of the kingdom to satisfy his personal needs, he chose not to.

The second temptation was not one of hunger, but one of protection. The devil urged him to jump off the pinnacle of the temple, summoning the protection of angels that surely would have come to his aid, preventing injury to himself. Again, no one would have blamed him if he chose to do so. But rather than use the full powers of the kingdom to heal and protect himself, he chose not to.

The third temptation was not one of hunger or protection, but of possession. The devil was offering him the kingdoms of the world, of which Jesus had a rightful claim anyway as the Lord over creation. None of us would have blamed Jesus for claiming rightful ownership of all creation. But rather than compromise the power of the kingdom and allow the tempter to win, he chose not to.

If there is one principle that emerges here as a sure remedy for temptation, it is this: Practice selflessness. Selfishness feeds temptation. Generosity and compassion overcome it.

Instead of turning stones to bread to feed himself, he would feed a hungry crowd on a hilltop. He saved his powers of healing and protection to heal those who were ill and dying. He saved his power to claim all creation until he could save the world and have others join him in glory.

Jesus passed the tests, and could then enter his public ministry focused and ready to do what he had to do. Likewise, this Lenten journey calls us to servanthood, combating temptation with a desire to glorify God and serve the needs of others.

Secondary Preaching Theme

If the Gospel text is about how to overcome temptation in the wilderness, the Old Testament lesson is about the promised reward for enduring the wilderness. Moses gives instruction to the Israelites on how to celebrate their long-awaited arrival in Canaan. He tells them to recount God's mighty acts of deliverance, and then calls on them to make an offering to God in gratitude.

Both of these elements—faithful remembrance and grateful response—should constitute the regular rhythm of a follower of God. Like the upbeat and downbeat of a song, or the systolic and diastolic pulse of a heartbeat, or the inhale and exhale of our breath, remembrance and response should be a part of the basic pattern of our lives.

The preacher might give illustrations of how God has brought deliverance to people throughout the congregation's collective memory, and invite moments for them to reflect on God's acts of compassion in their own lives. The observance of either communion or baptism on this day would be particularly appropriate, since both liturgies offer a recounting of God's saving acts throughout the biblical narrative.

There might also be an opportunity for joyful response in the service. Moses instructed the people to offer the "early produce of the fertile ground" that God had given them, and the congregation might consider creative ways to offer their best and fullest selves in service to God.

Prayer Application

God, thank you for giving us the strength to endure the temptations we face. You have not only empowered us to overcome them, you have also called us to self-sacrifice, that we might help others endure their suffering.

When we are tempted to turn stones to bread, help us to feed the hungry.

When we are tempted to isolate ourselves in self-protection, help us to minister to those around us who are most vulnerable.

When we are tempted to gain the world, help us to lose our lives in service to you, as part of your ongoing work to redeem the world. Amen.

Benediction

May you leave this place with the confidence that God is with you amid your wilderness. May you follow the wisdom of Christ, and follow his example of self-giving love. And may you be strengthened by the power of the Holy Spirit, who leads you into the promise of new hope. Amen.

March 17, 2019–Second Sunday in Lent

Passages: Genesis 15:1-12, 17-18; Psalm 27; Philippians 3:17–4:1; Luke 13:31-35

Gathering Prayer

God, we come acknowledging our fears and naming our longings. Grant us an awareness of your love, that we might return in faithfulness to you. Amen.

Preaching Theme

The Gospel lesson offers a different portrait of Jesus than the ones we are used to seeing. We are more accustomed to the powerful Jesus, who calms storms or raises dead people to life. Or the stern Jesus, who rebukes demons and reprimands Pharisees. But in this story, we see a Jesus who is longing and yearning.

"Jerusalem, Jerusalem, you who kill the prophets and stone those who were sent to you! How often I have wanted to gather your people just as a hen gathers her chicks under her wings. But you didn't want that."

You can almost hear the ache in his voice, because so many have experienced that longing themselves. Consider the parent who longs for wisdom and health for their wayward child, hoping they will someday choose the right path in life. Consider the married couple whose relationship is on the rocks as they both long for an end to the harm they are causing each other. And in this text, consider God, who has always longed for wholeness and peace for all of God's children yet sees how far they have fallen from experiencing either.

This text reminds us that human beings have been given the gift of free will; we are free to love and honor God, just as we are free to reject the way and will of God. God will not force us to choose the better way, for God does not operate with coercion. Instead, God works through persuasion, calling and luring us to return to a life of holiness and righteousness.

As Jesus was facing Jerusalem and beginning the week that would lead him to the cross, he came to a moment of profound recognition. Though he could perform miracles, conquer demons, and take command of the weather, there was one thing he could not do: he could not force people to love. Loving God and others is only possible through conscious choice. Otherwise, it is coercion and deception (at the very least) and harmful abuse (at worst).

At the end of the passage, Jesus gives one final warning: "Look, your house is abandoned. I tell you, you won't see me until the time comes when you say, 'Blessings on the one who comes in the Lord's name.'" Jesus reminds the people that their wayward choices come with consequences. Just as he cannot force them to choose the right path, the ramifications of those choices are often unavoidable. But even in those moments, when we wind up living in a mess of our own making, there can still be hope. God still offers the grace that can enable us to see God's saving presence in Jesus, and God is still working to redeem us and gather us in.

Secondary Preaching Theme

The Genesis text and the psalm have these two elements in common: they both describe the human response of fear, and they both affirm the strong protection of God as a counter to those fears.

It is true that the nature of Abram's and the psalmist's fear is different. Abram's fear was based on doubts that God could deliver on what God had promised him. The psalmist is surrounded by enemies (v. 6), and describes the condition of being encamped by armies and impending war (v. 3).

Yet both Abram and the psalmist discover that the antidote to fear is found in trusting in God. The congregation might have an opportunity to name their fears, their doubts, and the ways they feel "encamped" by terrors in their lives. Psalm 27 can then lead the congregation to a bold, unequivocal declaration of confidence in God, and an invitation to respond with joy amid struggle.

Prayer Application

O nurturing and compassionate God, you long to gather us into your heart and lead us into holiness.

O Fortress and Protector, you stand strong amid the tumult of life and are a bulwark, for our sure footing.

O Fount of Blessing and Love, you have made a covenant with us to be our God, and we your people.

O Word and Spirit, you inspire the psalmist to sing and the prophet to speak, and you call us to the way of joyful obedience.

O Light and Salvation, you vanquish our fears and set us high on a rock.

Grant that we might discover hope in your strength and a confidence to conquer our doubts that we might fulfill your deepest purposes in us and through us. May we join you in building your kingdom on earth as it is in heaven, that your offspring may be as plentiful as the stars in the sky and the sand in the sea. Amen.

Benediction

May you claim confidence in God's faithfulness and feel the warmth of God's compassion. And may you leave this place to be conduits of hope, in a world filled with fear. Amen.

"Christ the Hen"

Luke 13:31-35

Scott Hoezee

When I was a kid in the early 1970s, Saturday night meant watching my favorite TV show, *Emergency!* I loved that show about two brave paramedics from Squad 51 of the Los Angeles Fire Department. When Johnny and Roy were in danger, my pulse raced. Thanks to my father, who was a real-life volunteer fireman at the time, I even got an old fireman's helmet and painted a "51" on it so it would match Johnny's helmet. But I remember that one week on a Saturday night my parents went to visit with some friends in Holland, Michigan, and they took my brother and me along. The children of our friends were not accustomed to watching *Emergency!* and so come 8:00 p.m. that night, they turned on another show. I told them that my parents did not allow me to watch that particular show and so we should not have it on. The other kids relented, and soon I was nicely ensconced in front of their TV watching my heroes Johnny and Roy.

As it happened, it was not true that my parents did not allow me to watch that other show. I don't want to say I lied. It was more of what Winston Churchill once called "a terminological inexactitude."[1] But to hide my true motivation, I made up something that pointed to an authority figure whose influence would steer things my direction. "If we do this, you'll have to deal with my parents," I claimed.

I think that something exactly like that was behind the Pharisees' warning to Jesus about Herod's alleged plans to harm him. When we read this passage from Luke 13 a few moments ago, it should have struck you as vaguely surprising to see the Pharisees, of all people, huddling around Jesus so as to protect him from harm. After all, Jesus and the Pharisees did not exactly see eye to eye on most things. What's more, we're not too far away in Luke's Gospel from a time when the Pharisees will serve as Herod's *cheerleaders* in not just roughing Jesus up but actually executing him! So when we read that the Pharisees appear to be protecting Jesus in Luke 13, we have to conclude that either Jesus had finally run into a group of kinder, gentler Pharisees or something else is going on.

I think something else is going on and I suspect it's something devious. My hunch is that whether or not Herod was really taking note of Jesus and planning some harm for him, the Pharisees mention this to Jesus only as a way to get rid of him. In truth, it wasn't Herod who wanted Jesus out of Jerusalem; it was the Pharisees, the religious establishment. Jesus threatened so much of what the Pharisees stood for, as you can see in earlier parts of even this very chapter. He cozied up to the very sinners and tax collectors whom the Pharisees shunned. He told stories that, despite being a little hard to figure out, surely seemed to paint religious leaders in a bad light. In fact, the closer Jesus got to Jerusalem and to the very center of the temple establishment, the more threatened the Pharisees felt. Bad enough that Jesus caused a ruckus out in the sticks in Capernaum and Galilee but they could not afford to have him within the perimeter of the temple. That would strike too close to home. "Better get out of here," they said. "Herod means you harm." But it was the harm Jesus could cause to *them* that was their real concern.

In reply to this, Jesus says that although Herod is something of a fox, he wasn't going to let Herod chase him away or cause his work to cease. Twice in this passage Jesus refers to a three-day span of time—"Today and tomorrow and the next day"— which is a very Jewish way of referring to a significant event. Any time in the Bible where you read that such-and-such an event took three days, with the culmination occurring on the third day, you know it is something deeply meaningful. At this point in Luke 13 Jesus is not yet referring directly to his resurrection on the third day but seems to be saying that the whole course of his ministry bears such a huge significance that no one—not Herod, not the Pharisees, not the forces of hell itself—will ever derail him. Jesus never stops.

And no sooner did Jesus say that and he goes on to reveal a key reason why he would never stop: he has a heart as big as all creation. Jesus looks at Jerusalem, and his heart breaks. The Pharisees' attempt to chase Jesus off only added to the sadness Jesus felt for God's children. He was coming to Jerusalem to fulfill a ministry that would offer salvation by grace to all. But the closer he gets to it, the more people try to wave him off or chase him away. Indeed, when Jesus says in verse 32 that he will soon reach his goal, that word in the Greek is the word that means "to fulfill" or "to complete." The goal Jesus has is not some artificial finish line. Jesus's goal is the salvaging of all creation.

But the closer he gets to that goal, the more Herod the fox and those foxy Pharisees try to chase him away. Since he's surrounded by foxes anyway, Jesus decides to make the apt move of calling himself a mother hen. "Jerusalem, Jerusalem, you who kill the prophets and stone those who were sent to you! How often I have wanted to gather your people just as a hen gathers her chicks under her wings." Jesus never stops calling God's little ones to come to him, to come under the wings of his grace and salvation. He never stops. But the world keeps trying to stop him and sometimes, alas, the most religious people in the world try to stop him too.

To get their own way, the Pharisees pointed the finger at a secular figure like Herod, using his alleged threat to advance their own agenda. But the result was a fox-like chasing away of Jesus. This kind of thing happens. In fact, it keeps happening. The Pharisees' strategy isn't dead even in the church. How often do we hear loud cries from some church leaders about the threat represented by such-and-such a political figure, by this or that organization, by the so-called culture war or "the war on Christmas"? Some keep saying that it's the people "out there" who are the problem. But sometimes the longer and louder we say that, the more people "out there" feel like we don't want them "in here." And maybe that's partly true. By going on and on about this world's Herods, maybe what we're really trying to do is keep Jesus all to ourselves by chasing away those we're not sure about inviting in.

Maybe Herod really was making noises about roughing up Jesus. Maybe. But it wasn't Herod who ultimately made sure that Jesus got hoisted up on a cross. That grim task was taken up by the Pharisees and their ilk. They were the ones who made sure that the dear chicks whom Jesus wished to take under his loving wing never got anywhere near Jesus. The Pharisees were the ones who made sure that Jesus was made into such an ugly public spectacle that people hid their faces from him, whisked their children out of the way so they would not have to look upon the horror Jesus became.

But Jesus never stops. He never stops calling us to himself. He never stops lamenting all the lost "chicks" out there, and he wants them to come under the protection of his wings. What we should want more than anything is to help people hear the gracious invitation that comes ever and again from Christ the Hen. But do we? Do we make Jesus and his grace the focus of our energies and public testimonies, or do we tend more often to rail against our enemies and all those who disagree with us? When people listen closely to us, do they hear us waxing eloquent about Jesus and his love or complaining that science or the media or the government are out to get us?

These are not easy things for us to ponder. But then, Lent is a time to think about hard things. Lent is a time to see ourselves as the people who contributed to Jesus's pain, as the ones for whose sins Jesus died. And so Lent is a time to redouble our determination to leave our sins behind and stay in step with the Spirit as a response to the wonderful grace of Jesus that has caught up every one of us despite our ugliness, despite our sins, yes, despite even our attempts to prevent Jesus from doing what he came into this world to do: namely, to call all people unto himself.

As Luke 13 shows us, despite everything, Jesus never stops. In Lent and at all times this is something we see each time we gather at the Lord's table. Again and again Jesus calls us to himself, to fellowship with him in the holy supper. We are called each time to go under the wings of Christ the Hen. And that's really just another way of saying that we are being called home.

At a conference on the sacraments some years ago, N. T. Wright noted that according to John Calvin's theology, what happens to us in the Lord's Supper is that we really are elevated into the presence of Christ. Space, time, and matter coalesce in a deep mystery in which we really do go home to where Christ is at the right hand of the Father. We really do come under his wings when we respond to the invitation to come to the feast. For now, we do not remain there, but we glimpse and experience again the home that has been prepared for us by grace.

It's a glorious thing to be a chick under Jesus's wings. It's a glorious thing to know we have this home. That's why those of us who are blessed to be brought home to Christ the Hen need to go forth from his table to do all that we can to repent of any tendencies we have to chase chicks away from Jesus and to do all that we can to make sure that Jesus's soulful, compassionate, deeply loving invitation to gather God's chicks to himself is heard loud and clear by our neighbors, our coworkers, our friends, our family.

The Gospels tell us that the moment Jesus began his public ministry, he found himself in the wilderness being confronted by the devil. Jesus's ministry wasn't five minutes old before someone tried to stop him. The opposition never relented. But Jesus never stops. Foxes abound in Jesus's chicken coop. But Jesus never stops. He never stops. And so this day he calls you and me yet again. Tomorrow he wants to use us to call still more to join us at Christ's table in the future. He never stops.

Neither should we.

Amen.

March 24, 2019–
Third Sunday in Lent

Passages: Isaiah 55:1-9; Psalm 63:1-8; 1 Corinthians 10:1-13; Luke 13:1-9

Gathering Prayer

God, we gather this morning in your steadfast love, to sing your praise and bear witness to your grace. We come hungry, thirsty, and longing for clarity. Meet us in this moment, and transform us by your love. Amen.

Preaching Theme

We can admit that we are uneasy with the connection that both Jesus and Paul appear to be making between sin and suffering. In the Gospel reading, people asked Jesus to theologically explain why people had to suffer. They used as case studies two groups: the murder victims of Pilate and the victims of the destruction of a tower. In both instances, the questioners pondered a connection between their sin and their fate: "Did their sin cause their suffering?"

It is a conclusion that we would rather not consider, for obvious pastoral reasons. That's why Jesus's answer to the question is so disturbing. "Unless you change your hearts and lives," Jesus told them, "you will die just as they did." Does Jesus really believe that such suffering is caused by our sinfulness?

Fortunately, there is an answer to our uneasiness, in the parable of the fig tree. When the owner of the fig tree sees that the tree is bearing no fruit, he proceeds to do what any rational vineyard owner would do: cut it down and start over. That would be a reasonable cause and effect to assume. Sinfulness beckons punishment, just as fruitlessness beckons pruning.

But the gardener intercedes. He pleads with the owner to give the tree one more chance, appealing to the owner's heart of compassion to give the tree another opportunity for fruitfulness. He offers to provide extra care and nurture: digging around it to remove competing plant life and preserve water, and giving it nourishing fertilizer to give it the nutrition that it needs.

Jesus is the gardener in this story who steps into that gap between sinfulness and suffering in order to offer an irrational, unlikely second chance at life. If the stories of Pilate and the tower reinforce the natural consequences of our sins, then the story of the fig tree reinforces the certainty of God's grace. And in the end, it is God's grace and love, not the causality of sin, that rules the day.

Secondary Preaching Theme

The agricultural theme continues in the sayings of the psalmist and the prophet. Both texts open with a longing for water, a basic necessity for all living things to survive. Like the fig tree, the psalmist is feeling dried up and deteriorated, like a "dry and tired land." Yet, both the prophet and psalmist are able to claim joy because they see in God a chance at new life and grace. Isaiah attests to the higher ways of God that transcend the conventional wisdom of our broken world. We might question the nature of suffering and be challenged by other deep questions for which there are no easy answers. But God's ways and plans are higher than ours, and that promise can give us hope.

Likewise, the psalmist expresses confidence in God's strength, which enables the psalmist to speak praise with joy, and to cling to God with his whole being. The preacher might invite the congregation to make personal connections to both texts, asking them to consider how they feel like a dry and tired land, or how they feel thirsty and hungry, or how they are the wicked whom God is calling to abandon their ways and sinful schemes. Lent is a time for us to consider a sober assessment of our spiritual state, and both texts prompt such introspection.

But they both offer redemption in God's grace. The congregation might then be invited to consider how they have experienced God's love as "the richest of feasts" (Isa 55:2) or a "rich dinner" (Ps 63:5). The celebration of communion would be a natural connection to this imagery, inviting people to join together in the heavenly banquet that God has prepared for us in Christ.

Prayer Application

God, we come with questions for which there are no easy answers. Accept the limitations of our wisdom, and strengthen our faith.

We come hungry and thirsty for a fresh experience of your love. Feed us with the bread of life and the living water that satisfies us fully.

We come with callouses and bruises from long-standing suffering in mind, body, and spirit. Bind our wounds, grant us your healing spirit, and strengthen us for the journey.

We come acknowledging our sins, confessing them with earnest repentance. Grant us the second chances that only your grace can provide, that we might bear fruit for you. Amen.

Benediction

And now may the God who nourishes you with living water cause fruit to bloom through you, that God might feed a world that is hungering for new hope. Amen.

March 31, 2019–
Fourth Sunday in Lent

Passages: Joshua 5:9-12; Psalm 32; 2 Corinthians 5:16-21; Luke 15:1-3, 11b-32

Gathering Prayer

Sacred one, as we dive deeper into Lent, draw us nearer to you, O God. Remind us of your presence so that we may remember who you call us to be. Amen.

Preaching Theme

Luke 15:11b-32 is considered to be one long teaching moment by Jesus. It's helpful to remember that in the Greek, there are no punctuation marks. No periods, commas, and exclamation points. In order to translate a passage in Greek, the entirety of the text must be taken into consideration.

The prodigal son is one of the more fully developed parables that Jesus told. None of the characters are two-dimensional. All three express strong emotions in such a way that they invite readers to connect with them.

From the perspective of the elder son, it's the story of how he is steadfast and faithful while his feckless, prodigal brother squanders a fortune and is then welcomed home. From the perspective of the younger son, it's the story of how he foolishly asks for, receives, and then wastes his inheritance on dissolute living. Chastened and nearly starving, he realizes his father's servants are better off than he is, and so he formulates an apology and returns. From the perspective of the father, this is a story about losing a son and, in fact, regarding that boy as dead. It was very unusual that a son would ask for his inheritance before his father died, yet even knowing that this was not a wise choice on his son's part, the father acquiesces. In giving the inheritance to his son, the father shows surprising disregard for his own rights and honor.

The drama of this story takes off when the younger son practices his apology over and over. In it, he confesses his sin and recognizes that he has forfeited his position as son.

When the father sees his son across a field, he runs to meet him and we get a sense of hurried excitement. Some theologians wonder if the father is running to protect his son from scorn from his village. The father never seems to judge the sincerity of the younger son's confession and never waits for explanation. Instead, he orders slaves to "put a ring on his finger and sandals on his feet. And get the fatted calf and kill it."

Though honor and reputation were valuable commodities, the father again seems to care little for his own honor that was likely damaged through this incident. His joy is palpable.

And later, when confronted by the angry, hurt elder son, the father responds with compassion. He calls his elder son *teknon*, which means child. It is a form of affection that affirms their relationship. The father pleads with the elder son. He reminds him of their bond in verse 31: "[*Teknon*], you are always with me, and everything I have is yours." He tries to persuade him *to* accept his younger brother, "this brother of yours."

In the end, we don't know what the elder son chooses to do. Neither do we know what happened to the younger son. To be forgiven can catch us at our most vulnerable state. We have no ground to stand on; we simply accept.

Secondary Preaching Themes

Joshua 5:9-12

In the Joshua passage, pay attention to the Passover meal that the Hebrew people kept at Gilgal. What was the significance of this place and this meal? What is the significance of the transition from eating manna to food produced in the land of Canaan?

2 Corinthians 5:16-21

What are some of the messages of reconciliation that God has entrusted to us to share? Consider Paul's letter to the people in Corinth; focus on what it means to be reconciled to one another and to God.

Responsive Reading (Based on Psalm 32)

Happy are those whose transgression is forgiven,
Whose sin is covered.
Happy are those to whom the Lord imputes no iniquity,
And in whose spirit there is no deceit.
Let all who are faithful offer prayer to you;
At a time of distress, the rush of mighty waters shall not reach them.
You are a hiding place for me; you preserve me from trouble;
You surround me with glad cries of deliverance.

Be glad in the Lord and rejoice, O righteous,
And shout for joy, all you upright in heart.

Benediction

May the endless and unbelievable love of the Holy One speak to your heart today. May you experience God through the blessing of a relationship restored. May you experience grace that touches your heart and changes your actions. Amen.

April 7, 2019–Fifth Sunday in Lent

Passages: Isaiah 43:16-21; Psalm 126; Philippians 3:4b-14; John 12:1-8

Gathering Prayer

Lord of all creation, just as Mary anointed Jesus, anoint us this day with your Holy Spirit. Prepare us to serve and love and live in ways that give you glory. Open all our senses to all that you are doing. Thanks be to God. Amen.

Preaching Theme

Anointing can serve more than one function. You can commission a person as a witness, you can convey the Holy Spirit, and you can even pray for healing. The founder of Methodism, John Wesley, said, "The Gospel of CHRIST knows of no Religion, but Social; no Holiness but Social Holiness."[1] He went on to say, "You cannot be holy except as you are engaged in making the world a better place. You do not become holy by keeping yourself pure and clean from the world but by plunging into ministry on behalf of the world's hurting ones."

Let's look at the main people in today's scripture. The setting is rather simple: Lazarus's sisters are hosting a dinner for Jesus.

Martha

The only thing we know about Martha is found in verse 2. "There they gave a dinner for him. Martha served" (NRSV). Poor Martha. It may speak volumes that when her sister pours the equivalent of a year's wages onto Jesus's feet, Martha doesn't say a word. And Martha *not* speaking may reveal to us just how far she has grown since their last interaction. For Martha, literally serving Jesus, her family, and their friends is how she lived her life as an offering.

Lazarus

Lazarus is identified with what Jesus has done for him. Let's pause here for a moment.

What would our lives look like if we, like Lazarus, were identified first with what Jesus has done for us?

Lazarus is "one of those at the table with him [Jesus]." We know that Lazarus died and Jesus raised him from the dead. Aside from walking out of the tomb, we never hear Lazarus do anything. In all of scripture, he never says a word, never talks about what death looked like, or what it was like to be raised from the dead. What we do know is that Jesus loved him and that Lazarus welcomed him for dinner when he was in Bethany.

We also know that after Jesus had dinner with Lazarus's family, the Jewish leaders plotted to kill Lazarus because his life was a living reminder of the power of Jesus. Lazarus's greatest service to the gospel message was simply being loved by Jesus and living. He may not have done or said anything profound…but God used his life in amazing ways.

In our communities, we have people who battle addictions of all sorts. Some of these folks rely upon the support they get from Alcoholics Anonymous and Narcotics Anonymous. Many of their lives serve as a living reminder of the grace of God. Choosing life and facing your demons each day is a testament to God's faithfulness and love. And that, for some of us, is an incredible expression of service.

Mary served in a most unusual and personal way. While Jesus reclined at the table, she poured a pound of costly ointment on his feet, and then wiped them with her hair. Scripture says that the house was filled with the aroma of perfume.

When was the last time that you experienced the love and power of God in such a real way that you reeked from it? What would our lives "look like" if we bore the aroma of the Holy Spirit? What if grace and love and compassion poured out of us in an intoxicating way?

Secondary Preaching Themes: Isaiah 43:16-21; Philippians 3:4b-14

In the passages of Isaiah and Philippians there are incredible painted visuals. The prophet Isaiah paints a picture of seemingly contradictory images—rivers flowing through a desert. The Apostle Paul contrasts his story of privilege and early success with the deep and wide sacred value of knowing Christ that surpasses all of Paul's personal accomplishments. Consider how these secondary preaching passages focus on how God reconciles all things to God's self.

Responsive Reading (Based on Psalm 126)

When the Lord changed Zion's circumstances for the better, it was like we had been dreaming.

Our mouths were suddenly filled with laughter; our tongues were filled with joyful shouts.

It was even said, at that time, among the nations, "The Lord has done great things for them!"

Lord, change our circumstances for the better, like dry streams in the desert waste!

Let those who plant with tears reap the harvest with joyful shouts.

Let those who go out, crying and carrying their seed, come home with joyful shouts, carrying bales of grain!

Benediction

May the grace and love of Jesus be with you today. May you witness and experience God's grace in a real and transforming way. Just as Jesus was anointed, may your life be a blessing and anointing to others pointing toward the radical grace of Christ Jesus.

April 14, 2019–Palm and Passion Sunday

Passages: Isaiah 50:4-9a; Psalm 31:9-16; Philippians 2:5-11; Luke 22:14–23:56

Gathering Prayer

Sacred one, we come to you as people who are finishing our Lenten season. People who have fasted, abstained, and anticipated this holiest of holy weeks. Speak to us now your story of life and love. Open our hearts and minds as we open hands to receive your Holy Spirit and begin this Palm to Passion time of worship. Amen

Preaching Theme

On this Palm to Passion Sunday, the Lukan text has a great theme running through it that is hinted at, though never stated. As you explore Luke's narrative, notice that everything Jesus does is significant; every dramatic step makes his disciples stop and notice. They realize something is happening. They feel it. They know it. But they don't have a name for it.

What we see, as outside participants, is the cost of discipleship. During Passion Week, this motif seems to both culminate in and expand upon what has been happening in the entire book prior to this point.

In Luke's narrative, the word *disciple* is used frequently to describe the followers of Jesus. When we hear *disciple*, we might imagine the twelve disciples who followed Jesus. But *disciple* may also refer to the 70 and possibly 120 followers who took on the mantle of Jesus's teaching. A quick but important note is that Jesus accepted as his disciples women (Luke 8:1-3) and people whom others identified as "sinners," many of whom were not counted in these numbers.

And Jesus didn't just recruit disciples and then let them figure things out for themselves. Throughout the book of Luke, Jesus taught his disciples, giving them the kind of study-group learning experience many of us experienced in seminary. He explained the meanings of parables to them apart from the teaching he gave to the crowds (Luke 8:4-15). He sent them on mission trips without him and gave them authority to do the work of teaching and healing (Luke 9:1-6). He used them in crowd control when five thousand were fed (Luke 9:10-17) and shared a sacred moment at the transfiguration (Luke 9:28-36).

And so, during the final days of his earthly ministry, Jesus chose to utilize his disciples significantly to help them understand that their participation absolutely was wanted and needed. We know that they prepared the Passover meal and that Jesus told them, "I have earnestly desired to eat this Passover with you before I suffer." How is the ancient story of God's faithfulness from the time of Moses relevant then and drawing us to faithfulness today?

The story of Christ's passion expands into his trial, torture, and execution, and the cost of discipleship remains hinted at though never spelled out. Spend time in the text studying each key portion of Luke 22:14–23:56 from multiple perspectives: start with Jesus and then imagine how it unfolded to his disciples as well as those who might be listening and watching that are unnamed. In each section of this dramatic story, how and where is Jesus calling his disciples? What is the significance that Jesus chose his disciples during these defining moments in his ministry? Taking this home, in what ways are we as followers of Jesus his agents of love and grace every day?

Secondary Preaching Themes (Philippians 2:5-11 and Isaiah 50:4-9a)

Just as followers of Jesus in the Lukan passage are asked to reflect the cost of discipleship, here we find in the Apostle Paul's letter clear instructions on what it means to be a follower of Jesus. In the prophet Isaiah's passage, we see the wisdom of relying on God.

Responsive Reading (Based on Psalm 31)

I take refuge in you, Lord. Please never let me be put to shame.
Rescue me by your righteousness! Listen closely to me!
Deliver me quickly; be a rock that protects me; be a strong fortress that saves me!
Guide me and lead me for the sake of your good name!
Get me out of this net that's been set for me because you are my protective fortress.
I entrust my spirit into your hands; you, Lord, God of faithfulness—you have saved me.
You were intimately acquainted with my deep distress.
You didn't hand me over to the enemy, but set my feet in wide-open spaces.

Benediction

May the God of all creation draw you nearer as disciples of Jesus. As you slow down this week to take in the significance of Holy Week, remember that you are created for just such a time for this day and age. May your discipleship reflect the God of grace and mercy and passion. Amen.

April 18, 2019–Maundy Thursday

*Passages: Exodus 12:1-4, (5-10), 11-14; Psalm 116:1-2, 12-19;
1 Corinthians 11:23-26; John 13:1-17, 31b-35*

Gathering Prayer

Jesus, we come to you at this time from many places with many stories. Yet you know our struggles just as you celebrate our deep joy. Will you send your Holy Spirit to dwell amongst us as we worship so that we might take in the sacredness of your teachings this day? Come Lord Jesus, refresh us, challenge us, renew us. Amen.

Preaching Theme

When reading the Bible, especially stories that seem cut and dried like this one, some of the coolest things are found in the details that seem minor. In this case, it's not just that Jesus washed his disciples' feet; it's also *when* and *why* he did it.[2]

Jesus is preparing his people for their upcoming lives as disciples. During supper, he got up, took off his outer robe, tied a towel around his waist, poured water into a basin, washed his disciples' feet, and wiped them with the towel (vv. 4-5). The foot washing seemed to be going well until Jesus moved to Simon Peter.

Simon Peter couldn't get past the social violation of his rabbi doing the dirty task of a lowly servant. He couldn't get past Jesus touching his feet! When Peter finally begins to understand that this ritual of foot washing is symbolic of union with Jesus's sacrificial death,[3] he impetuously wants to be washed from head to toe. Peter doesn't get that the act of humbling oneself before another is the point. He doesn't get that there is nothing magical in the washing itself.

Foot washing is an act of aligning our actions with where we want our hearts to be. In washing their feet, Jesus intentionally chose an act that might be odd or uncomfortable to signify that choosing the wrong time for society might be the perfect time for justice. Living into the love, as we are commanded to show in John 13, means accepting justice and peace as an essential part of our reality.

We worship a God who will choose justice and peace in a time when it's often the least convenient. Just days before he is betrayed with a kiss by one of his closest followers, about twenty-four hours before the Passover meal, Jesus got up in the middle of their meal to teach us that foot washing is a symbol of our union with his life and death, and foot washing is also a sign of the community of faith.[4]

Jesus didn't just wash his disciples' feet as a one-time event. He clearly stated that the world will recognize our discipleship to Jesus in *how* we love one another.

And the world will recognize whom we worship not by how clean our clothes may be at the end of it all, but how dirty we are willing to get for the sake of the kingdom of God. Those who do not know Jesus's love may have a chance to recognize grace not by our eloquent words but by the ways our hearts that want to follow Jesus are in alignment with our hands that serve God's creation.

When Mary anointed Jesus's feet, the whole room smelled of perfume. So, when Jesus washed his disciples' feet, he was teaching them that the aroma of your discipleship is how you serve and lead. Because grace leads us to service.

Secondary Preaching Themes (Exodus 12:1-4, [5-10], 11-14; 1 Corinthians 11:23-26)

Exodus 12 recounts the story of the first Passover. Jesus celebrated the story of God's faithfulness from generation to generation with his disciples on this Maundy Thursday. First Corinthians 11 is one of the rare retellings of the sacrament of communion outside of the Gospel accounts. How does the width and depth of God's grace, present from generations long before our own, shape your understanding of this Maundy Thursday?

Responsive Reading (Based on Psalm 116:1-2, 12-19)

I love the Lord because he hears my requests for mercy.
I'll call out to him as long as I live, because he listens closely to me.
What can I give back to the Lord for all the good things he has done for me?
I'll lift up the cup of salvation. I'll call on the Lord's name.
Oh yes, Lord, I am definitely your servant—you've freed me from my chains.
**I'll offer a sacrifice of thanksgiving to you, and I'll keep the promises I made to the Lord in the presence of all God's people,
Praise the Lord!**

Benediction

May the aroma of your discipleship fill every room you enter. May the ways we respond, the ways we serve, lead, act, and react point to Jesus who has already given us everything we need for this world and this time. May the grace of our Lord Jesus Christ guide you and keep you this day and forever more. Amen.

April 19, 2019—Good Friday

Passages: Isaiah 52:13–53:12; Psalm 22; Hebrews 10:16-25; John 18:1–19:42

Preaching Theme

There is no doubt that we are surrounded by evil in this world. Injustice. Racism. Greed. Genocide. Human trafficking. Pride. Exploitation. Not only did our God leave heaven to make his home in this evil-filled world...not only did he stare evil in the face on a regular basis but on the cross of Calvary Jesus allowed himself to be cursed and afflicted by evil.

If we are too familiar with the scene, it may be easy for us to forget that, on the cross, something terrible was happening. A completely innocent man was brutally killed. The death of Jesus Christ was a beautiful tragedy. It was tragedy, because Jesus did not do anything to deserve such treatment. He was accused unfairly. He was sentenced unjustly. "He was pierced because of our rebellions and crushed because of our crimes" (Isa 53:5). Yet, Jesus's death was beautiful because of what it accomplished for us. Isaiah 53:5 goes on to say that "he bore the punishment that made us whole; by his wounds we are healed."

Because Jesus was betrayed, we have been treated with kindness that we don't deserve. Because Jesus was arrested, we have been set free. Because Jesus was denied, we have been accepted. Because Jesus was condemned, there is no condemnation for us. Because Jesus was mocked, we have been commended. Because Jesus was cursed, we have been blessed. Because Jesus was abused, we have been comforted. Because Jesus was dishonored, we have been honored. Because Jesus was beaten, we have been healed. Because Jesus's body was torn, we have confidence to enter the holy places of God. Because Jesus was forsaken by God, we have been welcomed by God. Because Jesus was killed, our lives have been spared. From Jesus's anguish comes our peace.

Secondary Preaching Theme

In John 19:26-27, we glimpse a powerfully human and, at the same time, wonderfully divine scenario. Jesus is hanging on the cross, with nails through his feet and hands. He has been beaten, crowned with thorns, humiliated, and mocked, and now he is struggling to breathe. In the throes of intense, gut-wrenching pain, Jesus *sees* his mother, Mary, and his beloved disciple, John. Oftentimes when we are in pain, all we can see is ourselves. We can't get out of our own situation even for a split second to be able to notice someone else. But the pattern of Jesus's life was clear. He was always seeing people. He saw the crowd like sheep without a shepherd. He saw Zacchaeus hiding up in the sycamore tree. He looked at the rich young ruler and loved him. He saw the woman with the issue of blood. And, while hanging on the cross, he saw his mother. In the midst of torturous pain, he was caring for others. Not only was he caring for his mother, but he was caring for those who were crucifying him. Remember his prayer, "Father, forgive them…"? And, he was caring for us too. Isaiah 53 says that it was our sufferings he bore. It was our punishment he endured.

Call to Worship

Come, worship Jesus, the one who was disfigured to the point of appearing inhuman.
Come, worship Jesus, the one who possessed no splendid form or desirable appearance.
Come, worship Jesus, the one who was despised and rejected.
He knows what it is to suffer, for he bore our anguish.
He knows sickness well, for he carried our infirmities.

Come, worship Jesus, who was pierced because of our rebellions.
Come, worship Jesus, who was crushed because of our crimes.
Come, worship Jesus, who exposed his life to death.
He was numbered with rebels.
He carried the sin of many.
He pleaded on behalf of those who rebelled.
Come, worship Jesus.

Prayer of Confession

It was my sin that you bore on the cross, Jesus.
It was my guilt, my shame, my infirmity, my anguish, my rebellion.
(Pause for a moment of silence.)
It is your blood that purges the deepest parts of me, Jesus.
It is your blood that ransoms me from my foolishness.
(Pause for a moment of silence.)
My hope is not in my own righteousness, but yours, Jesus.
I am safe inside your grace alone.
(Pause for a moment of silence.)
Thank you, Jesus.

Benediction

May you consistently draw near to God with the certainty of faith. Jesus has made a way for you. May you enter the holy of holies confidently because of Jesus's blood. Jesus has made a way for you. May you receive what is yours in Christ Jesus. May you live out every good thing that Jesus died to give you. Amen.

April 21, 2019– Easter Sunday

Passages: Acts 10:34-43; Psalm 118:1-2, 14-24; 1 Corinthians 15:19-26; Luke 24:1-12

Call to Worship

It is the first day of the week. Bring your doubts, your questions, and everything you do not understand with you to the tomb of our Lord Jesus Christ.
With unsettled minds, we come.
Bring the fears that cause your insides to tremble. Even when you are expecting the worst, you are welcome here at the tomb of our Lord Jesus Christ.
With anxious souls, we come.
Bring your emotions, no matter how raw. Look through the salty, stained-glass windows of your tears and see the empty tomb of our Lord Jesus Christ.
With our hearts overflowing with emotion, we come.
Stoop down and take a good look at the grave clothes that are neatly folded in the tomb of our Lord Jesus Christ. See two angels dressed in brilliant white, where the body of Jesus once was placed.
We see and believe.
In the middle of trying to make sense of it all, as you are grasping for some semblance of control, may you hear Jesus call your name.

Preaching Theme

Our God is very much aware of our humanness. Indeed, God created us as humans. Humanity was God's idea. What's more, our God knows *experientially* what it's like to be human. God became flesh. As the Son of Man, Jesus experienced suffering, peace, unfulfilled desire, relief, exhaustion, hunger, and thirst. He knows what it feels like to be alone. He is well-acquainted with grief. And, Jesus confronted death just as each of us will. As the Son of Man, he wished for a way around the suffering. As the Son of God, he submitted to the will of the Father and conquered death forever. Not only did God come to earth to do good and bring healing...not only was he put to death by hanging on a tree but God raised him on the third day.

Today, as we focus on the account of Jesus's resurrection, we recognize that the miracle of the Savior's new life is set against the backdrop of the disciples' humanness.

As humans, we fear. We are often afraid of what we can't control and what we don't understand. In Luke 24, some women went to Jesus's tomb with spices they had prepared. They went to do what they could to make the best of the difficult circumstances, but they found that the stone was rolled away and Jesus's body was not there. Not only that, but two men in dazzling apparel appeared to them. They reacted in fear, just as we would likely do. Notice that it is right in the midst of the women's fear that the word of the Lord speaks. The good news comes to them, not after they had figured everything out, but even as they trembled in fear. "He is not here. He has risen."

As humans, we forget. Jesus had told them before that he would be delivered into the hands of sinful people and be crucified. He had also told them that he would rise again on the third day. He had spelled it all out clearly for them. But, when it mattered the most, they didn't remember. They needed to be reminded; yet there, at the empty tomb, God's messengers did not shame them for forgetting. They reminded them gently, "Remember how he told you?" And, thanks to this gentle reminder, they did.

Secondary Preaching Themes

Death is a formidable enemy. Many people have a strong fear of death, for they can neither control it nor fully understand it. We don't know when or how we will die. We can't fully comprehend what happens when we die. Death is a mystery that is beyond us. But, the empty tomb testifies clearly that Jesus has destroyed death. Death is not beyond Jesus; instead, Jesus is above and beyond death! And, in Christ, we will all be made alive forever.

Responsive Offering Invitation

ALL: **Lord Jesus, rise again within me.**
READER #1: Let your Spirit breathe life into my sin-weary soul.
ALL: **Rise again within me.**
READER #2: Roll the stone away from my cold heart.
ALL: **Rise again within me.**
READER #3: I offer you my heart, willing and free.
ALL: **Lord Jesus, rise again within me.**

Benediction

As you leave today, may you go with the knowledge that the right hand of the Lord does valiantly. You will not die but live and you will tell of the work of the Lord. You have not been given over to death. Rather, you walk in newness of life because of Jesus's resurrection from the dead. May you announce to anyone who will listen what you have seen Jesus do and what you have heard Jesus say. There is power in your simple testimony.

April 28, 2019

Passages: Acts 5:27-32; Psalm 118:14-29 or Psalm 150; Revelation 1:4-8; John 20:19-31

Call to Worship

Praise the Lord! Praise God in his sanctuary!
Let every living thing praise the Lord!
Praise God for the incredibly great and mighty things he has done!
He has done great things for us!
Praise God with what you have.
We will praise God in this moment with everything he has given to us.
Praise God with all that you are.
We are holding nothing back, for God is worthy of our whole lives.
Let every living thing praise the Lord!

Preaching Theme

Our God is a God of extreme forgiveness. God does not simply overlook our offenses or pretend like they are no big deal. Extreme forgiveness offers hope for a new life to those who don't deserve it. In Acts 5:30-31, Peter and the apostles are brought into the presence of the high priest. Not too many months before, it was in the courtyard of the high priest that the chief priests and elders plotted to arrest and kill Jesus. It was the high priest's slave who, as part of the mob that came to arrest Jesus, got his ear cut off and later healed by Jesus. It was the high priest who declared Jesus was insulting God. The high priest himself incited the people to condemn, mock, and spit on Jesus. And the high priest had already arrested and imprisoned Peter twice for preaching and healing in Jesus's name. Peter has the opportunity to speak directly to the high priest and doesn't mince words. He declares in no uncertain terms that the high priest and those in his court were responsible for killing Jesus. He doesn't sweep the offense under the rug or pretend like it didn't happen. He tells it like it is. But, he doesn't stop there! In the same breath Peter declares that God is offering forgiveness for sins and the opportunity for a changed heart and life. It was in the courtyard of the high priest that Peter himself had sinned greatly by denying Jesus three times. But, because he had received extreme forgiveness, he was able to extend it to others, even his enemies.

Extreme forgiveness offers us a new future, with a new identity. Revelation 1:5-6 makes this extravagantly clear. Not only are we freed from our sins by Jesus's blood, but his blood makes us into something new! We are now a kingdom of priests to serve our God. Priests were able to freely enter into the holy of holies. The whole lives of priests revolved around ministering to God in the temple. We used to be enemies of God. Our sins kept us from his presence. Now, because of the blood of Jesus, we have become priests and we can enter freely into God's presence. Our lives are able to focus on serving and loving God forever.

Secondary Preaching Theme

Jesus responds graciously to fear and doubt. In John 20:19, we see the disciples hiding in a room because they were afraid of the authorities. Jesus comes right to where they are, stepping into the middle of their fear and hiding, and speaks peace. In John 20:25 Thomas doubts Jesus's resurrection, even though the other disciples tell him about their encounter with the risen Christ. Jesus does not shame Thomas for doubting or wait for him to overcome doubt on his own. Jesus steps into Thomas's doubt and speaks directly to him, offering an invitation to believe.

Prayer of Repentance

Though we do not deserve his grace, today, God offers us extreme forgiveness.
Forgive us our sins as we forgive those who sin against us.
We are set free from our sins by the blood of Jesus.
Forgive us our sins as we forgive those who sin against us.
God offers a new mind and a new heart.
Forgive us our sins as we forgive those who sin against us.
Will you forgive those who do not deserve your forgiveness?
Forgive us our sins as we forgive those who sin against us.
Will you trust that Jesus's blood is strong enough to free even your enemies from their sins?
Forgive us our sins as we forgive those who sin against us.
Will you offer hope for a new life to others?
Forgive us our sins as we forgive those who sin against us.
Amen.

Closing Prayer

God of extreme forgiveness, we thank you for not treating us as our sins deserve. We thank you that you have not written us off, but you offer us hope for changed hearts and lives. We thank you that you have a future for us in your kingdom. We thank you that you have made us new and that we can serve you with our whole lives. We pray that you would make us people of extreme forgiveness, ready to offer to others the grace that we have received from you. We pray this in the name of Jesus, Amen.

May 5, 2019

Passages: Acts 9:1-6, (7-20); Psalm 30; Revelation 5:11-14; John 21:1-19

Gathering Prayer

Eternal God, you are Alpha and Omega, the beginning and the end. You are the one who was, and is, and is to come. You are forever. We recognize that we live so much of our lives, spend so much of our time, focused on the temporary things of this world. Today, we choose to lift our heads to eternity. We choose to look away from perishable possessions, momentary concerns, and fleeting fancies. We look to you. You are the author and finisher of our faith. You are worthy of our attention and affection today and every day. Amen.

Preaching Theme

So much of this life is temporary. Very little lasts forever. Some things are quite obviously temporary, like hair coloring, vacations, mowing the grass, and middle school crushes. Phones, computers, cars, and even houses and governments wear out eventually. But some things are less obviously temporary. Sharing the gospel of Jesus with those who don't know him is temporary. There will come a day when missions and evangelism will no longer exist. There will come a day when there will be no more hungry people to feed, no more grieving people to comfort, no more death, pain, or tears. There will come a day when we, who have put our faith in Jesus Christ, will gather with people from every tribe, language, and nation around the throne and in that day, we will worship. Worship, indeed, is forever.

In Revelation 5:13-14, John catches a glimpse of eternity and shares it with us. In eternity, every creature in heaven and on earth—and not only that, but under the earth and in the sea—declares the glory of Jesus Christ, the Lamb of God. To make it even clearer that no one and nothing is left out, John says plainly, "I heard *everything everywhere* say,

'Blessing, honor, glory, and power belong
to the one seated on the throne
and to the Lamb
forever and always.'" (emphasis added)

We will worship forever because God always has been and always will be worthy of worship. Psalm 30 reminds us that he has rescued us from our enemies, healed us, and changed the very direction of our lives. He changed our mourning into dancing so that our whole being might sing and *never stop*! He will never stop being good, and so we will give him thanks forever. All the honor, glory, and power belong to him *forever and always*. So, we will praise God forever. Because God is forever worthy.

Take a moment to consider how much of your life you spend concerning yourself with temporary things. And, how much of your life do you spend investing time and energy in eternal things? What can you do this week to prepare yourself for eternity?

Secondary Preaching Themes

Posture is important. Saul was a proud and powerful man who was doing exactly what he thought was right. In fact, he was in the midst of actively persecuting God's people when a light from heaven encircled him. Interestingly, the first thing that changed was his posture. Acts 9:4 says that Paul "fell to the ground." He assumed a posture of humility and surrender.

In Revelation 5, John paints for us a picture of worship in heaven. Everyone is involved, singing, crying out in loud voices, praying, and playing harps. And yes, even bowing down. After a great crescendo of worship in which the angels, elders, living creatures, and everything everywhere declares the greatness of God, verse 14 says that the elders "fell down and worshipped." Though many debate who the elders are and what they represent, it is clear that they have a place of privilege in heaven. In fact, Revelation 4:4 tells us that they are normally seated on thrones that surround God's throne. Yet when the Lamb takes the scroll from the one who is seated on the central throne, the elders respond by falling down before the Lamb. They recognize that their own power and privilege could never compare to the greatness of God and the worthiness of the Lamb! And so, they take their rightful place in worship, a posture of humility and surrender.

What is the posture of your heart today? Are you willing to bow down before the brilliance and greatness of our God? Or are you choosing instead to hold on to your own pride and power?

Offering Invitation

Consider the one who is worthy of endless praise.
Consider the one who gives all people life, breath, and everything else.
Everything you have comes from him.
Every good and perfect gift comes down from the Father of lights. Consider him.

Consider the one who did not spare his Son, Jesus, but willingly gave him up for us all. Consider the one who bore your sin and faced death on your behalf.
Consider the one who *conquered* sin and death on your behalf.

What is your response?
What will you offer him today?
Bring your offering with a heart full of gratitude and worship.

Benediction

May you continually offer to God the worship that he deserves.
May you freely worship God in the here and now, wherever you may find yourself this week.
May you worship in each moment, no matter how frustrating or dark or comfortable it might be.
May your whole being sing and never stop worshipping God.
And may your heart be prepared for the forever worship that is to come.

May 12, 2019

Passages: Acts 9:36-43; Psalm 23; Revelation 7:9-17; John 10:22-30

Call to Worship (Based on Revelation 7:9-17)

Come, saints of the Lord, let us bow down and worship!
We come from every nation and tribe. We speak in different languages, yet we all worship one Lord.
Leader: We lift our voices with one voice saying:
Blessing and glory; wisdom and thanksgiving; honor and power and might be to our God forever and always.
For you have satisfied our hunger and quenched our thirst.
You have sheltered us from the scorching sun and refreshed us with cool springs.
You have clothed us in the white robes of the Lamb and dried our tears of sadness.
With outstretched arms we worship you. Blessing and glory be yours forever!

Preaching Theme

You will be my witnesses, Jesus had told the disciples in Acts 1:8. And indeed the book of Acts is a long record of how his statement was proved to be true. In story after story, the apostles, now empowered by the Holy Spirit, are now doing miracles similar to those Jesus himself had done. In the preceding verses (Acts 9:32-35) Peter, the one upon whom Jesus promised to "build his church," heals a man, Aeneas, who had been paralyzed for eight years. The language shares some overtones with Jesus healing the man who for thirty-eight years had been lame in John 5:1-9. Jesus says, "Get up! Pick up your mat and walk!" Peter uses the words, "Jesus Christ heals you! Get up and make your bed." Both men respond "immediately" to being healed.

Similarly, the context of Tabitha has echoes of the raising of Lazarus in John 11 and the raising of Jairus's daughter, the young girl in Mark 5:35-43. The death of Tabitha happens while Peter is in the area, but not present at the death (see Jesus's delay in getting to Lazarus in John 11:1-7); Tabitha is laid in "a cold place" (as Lazarus is laid in the tomb, John 11:38). In both stories mourners are present at the time Jesus and Peter arrive, and in both stories Jesus and Peter have them leave the area so they can pray alone at the bodies of the deceased (Acts 9:39-40 and John 11:30-36).

All the stories end with a full restoration of life. Jesus has told his disciples that they will do his deeds, and in the fullness and power of the Spirit, that's just what they do. We generally assume that raising the dead and healing the lame were God-given signs designed for the apostolic age. Most of us have no illusions that we are going to be physical healers to those who are physically dead. But perhaps we underestimate the degree to which God has empowered us to do more than we attempt. Jesus said, "I assure you that whoever believes in me will do the works that I do. They will do even greater works than these because I am going to the Father" (John 14:12). We must encourage ourselves and our congregations that now is not a time for us to shrink back but to lean forward. We are Christ's witnesses for this time and place! We have received the life-giving power of the spirit of the living God! Wherever we go death will not have the final word.

Secondary Preaching Themes

The Gospel of John is filled with narratives of conflict, many of which take place against the backdrop of a religious festival. Jesus has a contentious encounter with religious leaders during the festival of Hanukkah, the festival celebrating the dedication of the temple. As Jewish festivals go, Hanukkah was relatively new at the time of Jesus since it commemorates the rededication of the temple following the victory of Judah Maccabee over Seleucid control in the second century BCE.

Then as now, Jesus faced a divided crowd. While the common folk were intrigued, the religious leaders were suspicious. Regular people were so eager to believe in the goodness and mercy that motivated and animated Jesus's actions. Those miracles revealed a God who was merciful, kind, and good. This was the kind of God who would indeed raise the dead and heal the lame as the apostles would do throughout the book of Acts. But the religious leaders remained suspicious. They were more concerned that the authority of God was being moved from themselves and their traditions and teaching to the person of Jesus himself.

Confession

God of life, you offer us a good life: food to eat, friends to enjoy, and meaningful work to do.
Surely, you have led us into green pastures and directed us to still waters.
But we complain. For the table is set in the valley. And everywhere we look, we see death.
We fear the grass may not always be green; we worry the water may be dangerous. We are not sure if the path you set for us is the one we want to take.
We confess our fear, our worry, and our hesitance. We confess our lack of faith.
Help us to remember you are always by our side.
Leading us along good paths,
Protecting us with your love,
Offering us a good life.

May 19, 2019

Passages: Acts 11:1-18; Psalm 148; Revelation 21:1-6; John 13:31-35

Call to Worship

Hallelujah to your name, Lord Jesus! This morning shines in the light of your love.
The sun radiates your glory. The moon echoes your mystery. The birds sing your hymns and the trees clap their hands in praise to you.
For you have created this world to praise you.
Rain and clouds, beast and cattle, mountains and fields shout your name. Rocks and flowers tell of your power.
We, too, have been created to praise you. This morning may you open our dry lips and give us a fresh language of praise.
May we sing of your glory shining all around.
May we share in the external song of praise.
And may we, too, shine in the light of your love.

Preaching Theme

Walk into Earl's Kitchen, a restaurant on the north side of Chicago, and from the door you will be greeted with a larger-than-life–sized painting of blues singer Buddy Guy, crooning at you from fifty feet away. The image is big and explosively bright. It's only as you are led to your table that you realize that the picture of Buddy is actually made up of a composite of all his song titles arranged to form his image.

"Photo mosaic" refers to the way small pictures are arranged in such a way that they form a larger image. Each tiny square contains a fully formed whole (whether it's your face or the title of a Buddy Guy tune), a whole picture you could simply study and appreciate for its own characteristics. But when we step back, these individual segments create an entirely new scene.

Peter had received a piece of God's massive plan. The first piece was a disturbing dream that upended his categories of holy and profane. Followed by another: a nudge of the Spirit to follow the three unknown men who appeared unannounced at his door. The pieces just kept coming as Peter met a devout Gentile (who, in addition to having entertained an angel in his home, had also been receiving some pieces of his own: preaching, memories of Pentecost, recollection of a fragment of Jesus's teaching). Little by little, one piece after another, until it was clear: *even the Gentiles have received the repentance that leads to life!*

That's often the way it is with us too. We receive a piece of the bigger picture God is doing. It's a piece to meditate on in its own right, but it's often just a fragment of the bigger picture. We have a piece that must be combined with others to reflect the bigger picture of God's work in the world. Acts 11 is a call to both study the individual pieces the people of our congregation have been given and also keep stepping back to see how they fit into the larger whole. The particular assistance a church may offer to after-school tutoring programs or refugee resettlement is not only an opportunity to befriend and show Christ's love, it's also a window into a larger world of fragile communities and worldwide displacement. Helping our congregations make the connections between their experience and the bigger world is a movement toward the kingdom of the God who *so loved the world that he gave his only Son* (John 3:16).

Secondary Preaching Theme

The final sentences in the Bible speak of the complete restoration of all things. There is a coming day when the things of earth will be complete. What Paul once famously "glimpsed through a glass darkly" will blaze with clarity as humanity will now know not in part, but the whole. Those little pictures of God's intention passed along through the ages will finally compose the picture they have been arcing toward all along: The exquisite glory of the vulnerable Jesus. The Lamb of God upon the throne of love.

Responsive Prayer

Jesus Christ, you come to transform us and renew us in the image of God:
Shine in our darkness.
Jesus Christ, light of our hearts. You know our thirst:
Lead us to the wellspring of your gospel.
Jesus Christ, light of the world, you shine in every human being.
Enable us to discern your presence in each person.
Jesus Christ, friend of the poor:
Open in us the gate of simplicity so that we can welcome you.
Jesus Christ, gentle and humble of heart.
Renew in us the spirit of childhood.
Jesus Christ, you send your church to walk your path in the world.
Open for all people the gates of your justice and peace.

Offertory Prayer

Lord Jesus, all we have are gifts that have come from your hand. The gifts of time and energy, the gifts of work and play, the gifts of leisure and resources. We return them all to you through these tithes and offerings. Use them to build your kingdom of mercy and peace. Add our gifts to your kingdom's work of justice and love. So that your name may be praised and your glory be seen. It's in your name that we pray, Amen.

May 26, 2019

Passages: Acts 16:9-15; Psalm 67; Revelation 21:10, 22–22:5; John 14:23-29 / John 5:1-9

Opening Prayer

Let the people thank you, God!
Let all the people thank you!
Let the people celebrate and shout with joy. You judge the nations fairly and guide all nations on the earth.

Preaching Theme

The mysterious man of Macedonia (Acts 16:9-15) has long had a hold on the imaginations of people from southeastern Europe. The owners of my favorite gas station, for instance, have a large print of an olive-skinned man, arms outstretched and mouth open, seemingly pleading for help from the Apostle Paul asleep in the foreground. Just who is this man who appears to Paul in his dream? Some interpretations have suggested it is Jesus in the "distressing disguise of the poor"[1] as Mother Teresa puts it. At the time of Paul's dream, there was a lot for which to commend the people of Macedonia. They had been occupied by the Greeks and at the time of Paul's vision they were a proxy state of Rome. This vision changed Paul's ministry. He left immediately to the Macedonian town of Philippi. And he would subsequently travel to the towns of Thessalonica and Beroea. Paul never reveals whether he met the actual mysterious man of his dream. But we know that Paul's obedience to this vision led to the salvation of a merchant woman, Lydia, and to the liberation of a slave girl in Acts 16:16-19 and one of the most beloved stories in the book of Acts: Paul and Silas's miraculous release from prison in Acts 16:22-40.

One of the most powerful sermon illustrations I ever heard was from a man who was once the chief catalyst of World Vision. Preaching at LaSalle Street Church, he told the story of a young boy who desperately loved his aquarium full of fish. While the boy was away on vacation, the temperature gauge was mistakenly reset. Over the next few days the boy watched while one fish after the other died, unable to adjust to the warmer water. By the time the boy realized what was happening, it was too late to save the fish. "If only I had understood fish language! I would have heard them tell me it was too hot!" the boy wailed to his father. Paul received a vision with real words attached to it. He understood the people of Macedonia needed help. What about us? We have received real words too—from those losing their jobs in manufacturing plants who wonder where they will find work and those fearful they won't have health care; the pleas of a generation of young men of color and the worried voices of those concerned about law and order. "Please help us," they cry.

Secondary Preaching Theme

Self-agency is a large part of the Christian walk. Jesus recognized that immediately. The lame man by the pool of Bethesda is a good example. Before Jesus will heal him, the man must answer Jesus's question, "Do you want to get well?" While we are always to be open and responsive to where and how the Spirit guides us, it is also important to know *what it is we seek.* Augustine prayed, "Grant, Lord, that I may know myself as I know thee."[2] Paul knew where it was going and why. Jesus knew what his mission was and why. What about us and our church communities?

Benediction

Let God grant us grace and bless us; let God make his face shine on us.
So that the way of Jesus becomes known throughout the earth, and the way of God's salvation is revealed among all the nations. In the name of the Father, Son, and Holy Spirit. Amen.

June 2, 2019–Ascension Day

*Passages: Acts 1:1-11; Psalm 47 or Psalm 93; Ephesians 1:15-23;
Luke 24:44-53*

Call to Worship

Clap your hands all you people! Shout joyfully to God!
Sing praises to God. Sing praises! God is king of the whole world.
The leaders of the world are gathered before the Lord.
They clap their hands in praise.

Preaching Theme

This is the last moment of "real Jesus" the disciples have. It's the final physical contact the disciples have with their friend and Savior. (Though, since this is post-resurrection, I'm not sure if *physical contact* is the right way of thinking about it.) The text says Jesus had been with them for forty days, talking about the *thing he always wanted to talk about*: the kingdom of God (v. 3), while the disciples were talking about what *they always wanted* to talk about: *clarification*. The disciples wanted to know when the end of the world would happen and how it would happen and what would be the signs of the end. Then out of the blue, Jesus gives them his last instruction: "You are going to receive power and to be my witnesses in Jerusalem, in Judea and Samaria and to the ends of the earth" (v. 8)...and then disappears. They stand there—likely slack jawed and dumbfounded, looking up.

Every time I read this passage I have a flashback to Saturday mornings of my childhood. My dad would haul my younger brother and me in his battered yellow El Camino to these remote sections of our property—it felt like miles, but we only had fifty acres or so. We'd get out of the back and he would give us instructions on what we were to do—weeding, fertilizing, planting, painting—then he'd show us the way he wanted it done.

He would hand us our bucket of supplies and some water. Then he'd just drive off. He'd just *leave us*, expecting us to complete the work he'd left us to do by the time he would return. So I get, in my bones, why the disciples stood there gazing up at the sky, and why they had to be nudged into action. Because sometimes, *standing there* is just what you do, when you don't want to believe what's happening.

Jesus leaves the disciples with some unfinished business. Lots of it. It has taken me years to get this. Because for quite a while—even after I became a Christian—I kept thinking Jesus was going to finish the job himself. I think that's the impulse behind the disciples' clarification question in verse 6, "Is this the time when you will restore the kingdom to Israel?" (NRSV). They were planning on history coming to a close—but they were also planning on *Jesus wrapping it up.*

Instead of doing that, Jesus leaves them some tools ("You'll have power!"), gives them a job ("Be my witnesses!"), then gets into his truck and drives off, leaving thousands of miles of plain work in front of them. Endless fields to be seeded, planted, watered, and harvested. And he gives them one very small strategy piece: Start here, in Jerusalem, he says. Then, head west to the Judean towns, north up to Samaria, then just keep going—further and further out—until you reach the ends of the world.

Secondary Preaching Theme

Those seeking to emphasize the worth and importance of every believer need look no further than Paul's prayer for the people of Ephesus. Ephesians 1:15-23 speaks to the abiding value and priority God has placed on every one of us. If only we understood our beauty and our worth! Paul prays God's light will flood the darkness of our hearts so that we will know the greatness of God's power that is already at work in us and in our communities. Surely when Jesus leaves it is this power of God that he expects to be present in our work as witnesses.

Confession

Lord Jesus, we ask your forgiveness when we shrink back.
We don't feel we are up to the task you have given us.
We confess we worry more about what others are doing rather than what you have called us to do.
We don't know where to begin and we don't know if we can do what you ask.
But, Jesus, you have promised us that we will be your witnesses filled with the Spirit's power.
Help us today to put our fears behind us and do the work you have called us to do. So that your kingdom may come on earth as it is in heaven.

Benediction

May your hearts be filled with the hope of God's work in you.
May your minds be filled with the knowledge of God's love for you.
And may your souls be filled with the fullness of God's plan for you.

"After Ascension, Church"

Acts 1:1-14

Ted A. Smith

If there's one thing we know about Jesus, it is this: he is gone. Gone. Scripture, creeds, and cynics all agree. Jesus is gone. Our lesson from Acts gives details: "a cloud took him out of their sight" and "two men in white robes"—we might as well call them angels—attend the scene (1:9-11). Luke 24 gives the plain version: "he withdrew from them and was carried up into heaven" (v. 51 NRSV). The Gospel of John doesn't say much about Jesus's departure, but it remembers him talking about it all the time. "Do not hold on to me," Jesus says to Mary in the garden (20:17 NRSV). "I'm going away," Jesus tells the disciples (14:28). Different books tell the story in different ways, but everyone agrees: Jesus is gone.

The creeds of the church follow the witness of scripture. "He ascended into heaven," we say, in both the Nicene and the Apostles' Creed. He may sit at the right hand of the Father; he may come again in glory; but for us, for now, he's gone.

Here is one place where belief and doubt concur. "He's gone," the cynic says. "Well, isn't *that* a handy little doctrine? You say he rose from the dead. But where is he? He rose, but then he just flew up into heaven? Isn't that *convenient*?" Make sense of it how you will. But on this there is no disagreement: Jesus is gone.

✳ ✳ ✳

I believe all serious talk about the church happens in the wake of the Ascension. It begins with a recognition that Jesus is not with us as he was before. And this recognition of the absence of Jesus extends to a recognition of the truth about the church. For we confess that the church is the body of Christ. And we also confess that the body of Jesus is gone, absent, ascended into heaven. To say that the body of Jesus is gone is to say that whatever else it is, the church is not *identical* to Jesus. This is not a point of abstract doctrine. It is the deep, faithful, painful recognition that our congregations, parishes, and denominations are not as they should be. It is a confession that the church has repeatedly failed to give its life for the lives of others, as Jesus did. It is an acknowledgment that—again and again, in every century—the church has failed to transcend the divisions of nation, race, class, and politics that cut across the globe. It is a recognition that church bodies have too often been conformed to this world rather than transformed by the Holy Spirit. Again and again, the church demonstrates that the body of Christ is gone. We would not tell the truth if we said anything else.

✳ ✳ ✳

Nor would we tell the truth if this was *all* that we said. The Gospel of John, especially, reminds us that the going of Jesus is inseparable from the coming of the Holy Spirit. "I will not leave you orphaned," Jesus says to the disciples. "I am coming to you" (14:18 NRSV). He promises them the gift of Advocate, Paraclete, Comforter. Jesus ascended, Ephesians says, "so that he might fill all things" (4:10 NRSV). John Calvin has these passages in mind when he writes,

> Carried up into heaven, therefore, he withdrew his bodily presence from our sight, not to cease to be present with believers still on their earthly pilgrimage, but to rule heaven and earth with a more immediate power. But by his ascension he fulfilled what he had promised: that he would be with us even to the end of the world.[1]

Jesus is gone. And the Spirit of Jesus has come, to fill heaven and earth with an even more immediate and intimate power, that Jesus might be with us always, even to the end of the age.

✳ ✳ ✳

Stay with me now: there's one more move in unfolding this dialectic by which we live. Jesus is gone, the Holy Spirit has come ... and still, more than ever, Jesus is gone. The persons of the Trinity are not interchangeable parts. They are not fungible goods. The Ascension is not like some cosmic change machine, in which we put a dollar bill in, get four quarters back, and trust that it all spends the same. We can't lose Jesus, receive the Holy Spirit, and move along as if we had lost nothing at Calvary.

Canadian theologian Douglas Farrow says it like this: "Pentecost does not *resolve* the problem of the presence and the absence. It *creates* it, by adding a presence which discloses an absence."[2] Without the gift of the Holy Spirit, we don't even know what we are missing. It is the presence of God in the church that lets us see the absence of God from the church. This is what I mean: it is exactly at the communion table, when God gives Godself to us most deeply, when we taste and see that the Lord is good—it is just *here* that we feel the distance of the church from God most deeply. It is as we gather around the table that we feel the absence of those many thousands gone, those enslaved bodies, those gay and lesbian bodies, those sick bodies, those criminal bodies, those poor bodies, those bodies declared illegal, that crucified body of Jesus ... *all* those bodies—sometimes our own bodies!—that we have tried to stuff under the table and into the closet, just out of reach of our memory. The presence of God reminds us of their absence. In the presence of God, they cry out—we cry out—with the souls under the altar (Rev 6:9-11).

✳ ✳ ✳

Imaginations formed by the Ascension can think—can *live*—presence and absence together. It is important to see here that presence and absence don't strike a little deal, dividing the church between them, with presence getting these parts where things seem to be going as they should and absence getting those parts where we fall short. There is a deeper dialectic at work, and it runs through every corner of church life.

Thus imaginations formed by the Ascension can say no to visions of unqualified presence. They can dwell in the space of Holy Saturday, not rushing to the closure of Sunday's Alleluia. They can hold open the space for deliberation in the meantime, the in-between time, and so refuse the easy comforts of false fulfillment.

Imaginations formed by the Ascension also say no to unqualified absence. They refuse the dime-store despair that sees only power politics at work in the church. They refuse the cheap cynicism that says things will never change. And they refuse the hubris that says it is all up to us. If they do not rush to Sunday, they also refuse to understand the Saturday in which we dwell as anything but the day between Good Friday and Easter Sunday, the day made possible by the presence God surrenders at the cross on Friday and the day already transformed by the resurrection presence God gives on Sunday. Imaginations formed by the Ascension refuse any vision of absence that forgets that it is bracketed, disclosed, *within* the presence of God.

Christians in the wake of the Ascension see both presence and absence. We are called to sit in the dark of absence long enough that, in Howard Thurman's glorious phrase, we see the *luminous* qualities of the darkness.[3] This kind of faith does not involve finding a bright spot here or there. It comes as we see the ways that God is present in and in spite of the depths of sin and despair. For it is only by the power of God that we can name these things for what they are. They might present themselves as worthy of our trust, the only option if we want to live, but the luminous darkness reveals that they are not. They might present themselves as eternal, but in the luminous darkness we can see that trouble does not last always. Dwelling in the luminous darkness after Ascension lets us see things as they really are. It involves receiving enough of the presence of God in the life of the church that we can't let go, then finding ourselves broken open by the depth of the absence that presence discloses . . . and then finding ourselves, in that breaking, bound yet more tightly to the one broken for us.

Ascension faith has the tenacious patience to wait for the present fullness of Jesus's resurrection. It can say no to the offer of every alternative, every other power that promises it can sustain the church. It can refuse every other source of community as false. It can say no to peace built on agreement about how to vote, or whom to ordain, or how to interpret scripture, or what kind of worship we prefer. Ascension faith has the courage to refuse alternatives like these. It has the tenacity to wait for the peace of Christ by the peace of Christ. Ascension faith has the capacity to *yearn.* It knows how to yearn for the risen body that we trust will come again.

✳ ✳ ✳

At the end of today's lesson the "men of Galilee" are left staring into space. They have seen the body of Jesus ascend, and they are just waiting for him to come back. And the angels say, "Don't just stand here looking at the sky, contemplating the dialectic between presence and absence. Jesus will return to you in the manner in which he left." That is, he did not leave because you sent him away, and he will not return because you tell him to come back. Jesus will return when he will, because he so wills. Because of love. The men of Galilee seem to get it for a change. They do not stay to gaze into the sky. They come down from the mountain. They go back to the work of being church, back to yearning. They go back to the luminous darkness of the upper room, back to the place the women have been all along. I like to think of them sitting together, breaking bread, saying prayers, and sharing possessions, there, in that upper room that they shared with Jesus, a place that he once filled so richly that they must feel his absence keenly now…there, in the luminous darkness of that absence, being the body of Christ as they wait for the body of Christ to come again in glory.

June 9, 2019–Pentecost Sunday

Passages: Acts 2:1-21 or Genesis 11:1-9; Psalm 104:24-34, 35b; Romans 8:14-17 or Acts 2:1-21; John 14:8-17, (25-27)

Call to Worship (Based on Psalm 104:24-35)

Lord, you have done so many things! The earth is full of your creations!
Let my whole being bless the Lord! Praise the Lord!
All your creations wait for you to give them their food on time. When you let loose your breath, they are created and you make the surface of the ground brand-new again.
Let my whole being bless the Lord! Praise the Lord!
I will sing to the Lord as long as I live; I will sing praises to my God while I'm still alive. Let my praise be pleasing to him; I'm rejoicing in the Lord!
Let my whole being bless the Lord! Praise the Lord!

Assurance of Pardon (Based on Romans 8:14-16)

Sons and daughters of God, you are no longer slaves to sin and fear but you received a Spirit that shows you are adopted as God's children. With this Spirit, we cry, "Abba, Father." This Spirit assures us that we are God's children.

Preaching Theme

I have wondered for some time if we should understand God's actions at the tower of Babel finally as actions of judgment or grace. The people in this story used their common language to "make a name for [them]selves," and perhaps even to avoid God's original command to humanity to fill the earth (Gen 1:28). It's almost as if God is intimidated by the power of a people united in language and purpose ("nothing they plan to do will be impossible for them"), and so God scatters them by confusing their language. They were doing something wrong, and God stopped them by doing two things: confusing and scattering. These hardly seem like actions of grace.

This story gives an account of the diversity that we encounter, and it seems at first that this diversity is a punishment. Language is, of course, just the tip of the iceberg. *But* have we not come to understand diversity as a gift? Who laments the rich diversity of languages spoken across the world? Who laments the rich diversity of experiences and traditions that these languages communicate? Yet it seems that when it's left up to us, we congregate near the people who are most like us, who speak the same language, have the same Christmas traditions, and drive the same minivans or pick-up trucks. So perhaps we might come to understand God's actions at the tower of Babel as a kind of grace. There is confusion at first, certainly, but God's good intentions for humanity unmistakably include diversity despite our best efforts to stick with those most like us.

How appropriate, then, that the actions of God on Pentecost affirm God's resolve to promote diversity of language and experience. The spirit of God does not belong to one language group, social class, gender, or age group. Through the lens of Pentecost we can come to understand that God's acts at Babel are not the antithesis to grace, but perhaps finally a means of grace.

Secondary Preaching Themes

The Holy Spirit does not erase differences among language groups, social classes, genders, races, or age groups—the image of a melting pot won't work here!—yet there is a sense of unity between these diverse groups because of the Holy Spirit. The Holy Spirit enables each group to hear and speak of the mighty acts of God (Acts 2:11). The Holy Spirit is a companion, or advocate, to all believers who constantly reminds us of Jesus's words (John 14:26). The Holy Spirit unifies all believers as the one who brings about our adoption into the family of God and then testifies to our own spirits that we really do belong (Rom 8:14-17). These works of the Holy Spirit make unity in diversity a possibility.

It is easy and natural to be dismissive when people begin acting in unexpected ways, perhaps even more so when God seems to act in unexpected ways. The Pentecost event that amazed some left others with a dismissive look of haughty disdain on their faces: "They're full of new wine," or in other words, "They must be drunk" (Acts 2:13). This same response is alive and well in the church wherever marginalized voices are quickly dismissed for being too libertine, too feminist, too inclusive, and so on. Being dismissive of challenging views is certainly easier than engaging them, but this dismissal comes with a great risk as well. The risk of dismissing and silencing such voices is that we would miss the prophecy, visions, and dreams that the Holy Spirit has given to sons and daughters, young and old, of all races and social classes.

Benediction (Based on John 14:25-27)

Go with this blessing of Jesus: "Peace I leave with you. My peace I give you. I give to you not as the world gives. Don't be troubled or afraid." We go in this peace. Amen.

June 16, 2019–Trinity Sunday

Passages: Proverbs 8:1-4, 22-31; Psalm 8; Romans 5:1-5; John 16:12-15

Assurance of Pardon (Based on Romans 5:1-5)

People of God, you have been made righteous through the faithfulness of our Lord Jesus Christ. Through Jesus Christ you have peace with God. Now stand in God's grace; here you will find hope in your troubles as the love of God is poured out in your hearts through the Holy Spirit. Thanks be to God.

Prayer for Illumination (Based on John 16:12-15)

Come, Holy Spirit. Be among us now and guide us into all that is true. Proclaim your good word among us that we might glorify you—Father, Son, and Holy Spirit.

Preaching Theme

Psalm 8 sets up an understanding of human existence and purpose that is God-centered rather than human-centered. The body of the psalm is about human dominion, but it is bookended by direct praise to God and even the body is directed to God and carries a tone of praise. So the question of human existence and responsibility—how did we get here and what are we good for?—is perhaps a question that is best answered when praising God.

Praising God, as the psalmist does, will simultaneously produce a sense of humility and great honor when we consider our place in the world. The psalmist looks to the moon and the stars, but we can even look beyond that to other planets and galaxies and black holes and deep mysteries of "the heavens." God's glory is higher still. The view of earth from neighboring planets, let alone neighboring galaxies, does indeed make it nearly impossible to believe that the creator would care so deeply for humanity. Praising the creator God should invoke a deep sense of humility. On the other hand, the psalmist praises God because, despite how ridiculous and impossible it seems, God has crowned humans with glory and grandeur. What's more, this glory and grandeur comes with the honor of ruling over God's handiwork. Praising God will invoke a deep sense of humility *and* honor.

Praising God will also remind us that, though we have been given a degree of power and responsibility over creation, we are not free to exploit creation. Praising God helps us to better understand the role humans are given. "Ruling" over creation is a gift; it is something given to us by the creator—a royal task that is assigned to us for the benefit of creation and not our own benefit. We would do well to model our care for creation after the wisdom of the creator whom we worship. Proverbs 8 describes the creator's wisdom in creation as "having fun, smiling before him all the time, frolicking with his inhabited earth" (8:30-31a). Creation care is a weighty and difficult task, but as we praise the creator, we may also begin to delight in our task as caretakers of God's good creation.

Secondary Preaching Themes

If our understanding of human existence is framed in terms of God's majestic name, as it is in Psalm 8, then Trinity Sunday gives a wealth of vivid images that help us fill in that picture of God's majestic name. Proverbs 8 paints a picture of God's majesty that includes power over the forces of chaos in creation, but it also paints a picture of having fun, smiling, frolicking, and delighting. We no longer picture God as an austere, powerful king sitting on a heavenly throne somewhere high above us, but God's wisdom in creation looks more like my toddler who is happiest outside in the dirt and sand.

Romans 5 paints a picture of God's majestic name that includes Jesus Christ and the Holy Spirit. In royalty terms, Jesus Christ is the one who introduces us to the monarch because we cannot enter the monarch's presence on our own terms. Jesus is the "introducer" who brings us into the presence of the God of grace. The Holy Spirit is pictured as the conduit of God's love who pours God's love into our hearts. It is the Holy Spirit's reliable actions that ensure our hope.

John 16 pictures the Holy Spirit as a guide who helps us navigate what is true and what is yet to come. Any of these images could be helpful for filling out our picture of God's majestic name on Trinity Sunday.

Collect Prayer (Based on Psalm 8)

Lord, our Lord,
who set the moon and the stars in place,
give us wisdom to rule over the works of your hands—the flocks and herds, birds and fish,
so that we might reflect your glory and delight in creation.
Lord, our Lord, how majestic is your name in all the earth.

June 23, 2019

Passages: 1 Kings 19:1-4, (5-7), 8-15a; Psalms 42 and 43; Galatians 3:23-29; Luke 8:26-39

Prayer (Based on Psalms 42-43)

Just like a deer that craves streams of water,
my whole being craves you, God.
My whole being thirsts for God, for the living God.
When will I come and see God's face?
For those whose tears flow freely,
for those who are taunted by doubt:
God, give them hope.
For those who are weighed down by depression,
for those whose souls are heavy:
God, give them hope.
For those whose bones are crushed under the burden of oppression:
God, give them hope.
For those who suffer injustice,
for those who fear rejection:
God, give them hope.
Let us come to God's altar—
let us come to God, our joy, our delight.
Why, I ask myself, are you so depressed?
Why are you so upset inside?
Hope in God!
Let us again give him thanks,
our saving presence and our God.

Assurance of Pardon (Based on Galatians 3:23-29)

Now that faith has come, you are no longer guarded under the law. Now you are all God's children through faith in Christ Jesus. All of you who were baptized into Christ have clothed yourselves with Christ. There is neither Jew nor Greek; there is neither slave nor free; nor is there male and female, for you are all one in Christ Jesus. You belong to Christ.

Preaching Theme

Where I went to seminary I think it must have been a prerequisite requirement that every entering student love J.R.R. Tolkien's *Lord of the Rings*. I was no exception to that rule, but even to this day I cannot read the books or watch the movies by myself in the dark. And that's because of Gollum; Gollum makes my skin crawl. His presence in the movie gets me looking suspiciously at my dark closet and peering only cautiously outside my window into the dark for fear of seeing his hunched, translucent body and hollow, crazy eyes looking back at me. He reminds me of everything that creeps under the ground, everything that hides in caves away from the light.

This is how I picture the demon-possessed man in Luke 8, and I imagine my reaction to Gollum is similar to the way people reacted to the man in this story. He creeps in their caves and lives among their dead. He sleeps on the shelves carved out of the stone where bodies lie to decompose. His clothes have long disintegrated and his eyes have grown wild in the darkness.

When Jesus comes to the region of the Gerasenes, he is a perfect stranger to the Gentiles living there. To the average person there is nothing spectacular about his appearance as he steps off the boat. But to the man who lives in the darkness, Jesus looks as bright and feels as hot as the sun. The man is overwhelmed with fear and falls to the ground. The light of the Son of God drives out the destructive power of this legion of darkness. The man is given a new life, but the large herd of pigs is destroyed by the darkness. As a result, Jesus is the cause of great fear among the townspeople. Instead of seeing the hope of new life—the crazy man, now dressed and in his right mind sitting at Jesus's feet—the people only see the carnage of the darkness. The healed man wants to leave with Jesus, but Jesus insists that he stay among his people as a witness, or a seed of Jesus's gospel of deliverance and light. "Return home and tell the story of how much God has done for you," Jesus tells him.

This story is our story; though we may not have been possessed by a legion of demons, many of us know what it's like to live in isolation and darkness. Jesus has entered the caves of death, and his body has been laid on the shelves carved out of stone where bodies lie to decompose. When Jesus left the cave he brought all those in darkness with him, including us. Now we share the same imperative, "Return home and tell the story of how much God has done for you."

Secondary Preaching Theme

The image of a cave is present in 1 Kings 19 as well. When Elijah finally reaches Horeb, he spends the night in the cave. He receives a word from the Lord while he's in the cave, and it is a "thin, quiet" sound—no doubt a sound of peace compared to the wind, earthquake, and fire that preceded it—that draws him out of the cave into the Lord's presence. As in the story of Luke 8, God comes peaceably, not in chaos or destruction.

Sending

We are sent out with the same instructions Jesus gave the man after he had been healed and given a new life: "Return home and tell the story of what God has done for you."

June 30, 2019

Passages: 2 Kings 2:1-2, 6-14; Psalm 77:1-2, 11-20; Galatians 5:1, 13-25; Luke 9:51-62

Call to Worship (Based on Psalm 77:11-13)

Let us remember the Lord's deeds;
Yes, we will remember your wondrous acts from times long past.
Let us meditate on all your works;
We will ponder your deeds.
God, your way is holiness!
No one is as great as you, God!

Call to Holy Living (Based on Galatians 5:1, 22-25)

Christ has set us free for freedom.
Now, if we are guided by the Spirit then we won't carry out selfish desires, which are against the Spirit.
Instead, let us exhibit the fruit of the Spirit: love, joy, peace, patience, kindness, goodness, faithfulness, gentleness, and self-control.
There is no law against things like this.
Those who belong to Christ have crucified the self with its passions and its desires.
Now that we live by the Spirit, let us follow the Spirit.

Confession (Based on Galatians 5:1, 19-21)

Christ has set us free for freedom.
Yet, we confess that we are often willing slaves of our own selfish desires.
We willingly and selfishly indulge in sexual immorality, moral corruption, and doing whatever feels good.
We set up false idols that demand our obsession, and that revel in conflict, selfishness, anger, and group rivalry. We get drunk on jealousy and hate.
God, forgive us.
Guide us by your Spirit so that we will no longer carry out these selfish desires.

Preaching Theme

If the preschool, toddler, and children's Bibles in my house are any indication, 2 Kings 2 will be best known for the image of fiery chariots coming down from heaven to swoop up Elijah in a windstorm. This is undoubtedly a remarkable and vivid image. However, an overemphasis on this image may miss the main point of this story. Second Kings 2 is primarily interested in telling the story of prophetic succession, and the ascension of Elijah is just part of it. Throughout the passage, Elisha resolutely follows his master, Elijah, despite being told multiple times to stay put. Elisha's request to Elijah for "twice your spirit" refers to the double portion of the inheritance that legal heirs would receive (Deut 21:15-17), so he is not asking for twice the prophetic spirit of Elijah so much as he is asking to be Elijah's successor equipped with the same prophetic spirit. Elisha will not leave his master's side until he has been equipped with the spirit equal to his prophetic task. Elijah recognizes that this is not a request he has the power to meet, but if Elisha sees Elijah being taken from him, then it will be a sign that God has granted Elisha his request.

After Elijah is taken up to heaven in a whirlwind, Elisha picks up Elijah's coat and divides the water of the Jordan so he can walk across on dry ground. This is a sure confirmation that Elisha has received the mantle of Elijah's prophetic leadership—it is a reenactment of the same thing Elijah had just done. This prophetic miracle may be the answer to Elisha's anguished cry, "Where is the Lord, Elijah's God?" The answer, shown in Elisha's power to part the water, is unmistakably, "The Lord's spirit is here, resting on you, Elisha." "Elijah's God" has equipped Elisha for his prophetic task.

Secondary Preaching Themes

There are unmistakable parallels between Elijah/Elisha and Moses/Joshua in the exodus story. Elijah's coat and Moses's rod are symbols of their authority and power, and by this authority, both leaders divide water and walk across on dry land. Elijah, like Moses, has left the earth without a burial site (Deut 34:5-6) and departed in the same region—having just crossed the Jordan. Elisha and Joshua, respectively, replicate the miraculous parting of the waters as a sign that the prophetic authority of their predecessors has been passed on to them. Psalm 77:20 assures us that it is God who is leading his people through the waters with these prophets.

Luke 9:51-62 mirrors Elijah's journey before his ascension. Whereas Elisha followed Elijah resolutely, Jesus seems aware that his disciples and other would-be followers are not exactly up to the task, or at least that they have misunderstood his task. There is fire in this story too, at least the suggestion of heavenly fire, but Jesus's journey to his Ascension will not take him *around* death or opposition; it will take him straight *through* death. But after Jesus's resurrection and before his Ascension, he does what Elijah was unable to do: he promises his disciples that they will indeed receive a double portion of his Spirit. That is to say, they will be his prophetic successors and they will be equipped with the Spirit equal to their prophetic task of witnessing to the world.

July 7, 2019

*Passages: 2 Kings 5:1-14; Psalm 30; Galatians 6:(1-6), 7-16;
Luke 10:1-11, 16-20*

Call to Worship (Based on Psalm 30)

You who are faithful to the Lord, sing praises to him;
Give thanks to his holy name!
His anger lasts for only a second, but his favor lasts a lifetime.
Weeping may stay all night, but by morning, joy!
You changed my mourning into dancing.
You took off my funeral clothes and dressed me up in joy
so that my whole being might sing praises to you and never stop.
Lord, my God, I will give thanks to you forever.

Preaching Theme

Sometimes God asks us to do weird things: a prompting to talk to that stranger, a commitment to a local body of believers, even a call to ministry! How much easier it would be if God always made sense but God, it seems, has a different plan and purpose. And the question is, can you wade into uncertain waters even when you're not sure how it'll turn out? Can you trust God's plan even when you don't see the purpose?

Trust is a central theme in the story of Naaman. The trust of a servant girl who knows exactly what to do: send him to the prophet in Samaria. The foreign king who trusts enough to say, "Sure. Give it a shot and here's a letter of safe passage." The king of Israel who doesn't trust and freaks out that what is being asked of him is beyond his capacity. Elisha, the man of God, who said, "Why didn't you trust? I can do this." Naaman who mistrusts the answer he gets. "But Naaman went away in anger. He said, 'I thought for sure that he'd come out, stand and call on the name of the Lord his God, wave his hand over the bad spot, and cure the skin disease. Aren't the rivers in Damascus, the Abana and the Pharpar, better than all Israel's waters? Couldn't I wash in them and get clean?' So he turned away and proceeded to leave in anger" (vv. 11-12). The servants who chase Naaman down and convince him to give it a try.

Notice, too, that the ability to trust demonstrates a reversal of power in this narrative: servants and a foreign king rank high in trust whereas the king of Israel and the commander of the army (clearly more comfortable giving than receiving orders) distrust themselves, God, and the plan set before them.

Secondary Preaching Theme

Psalm 30 tells the story of someone who, when everything is going well, forgets to trust in God and depends, instead, on his own sense of security. That proves faulty ground, however, and the psalmist's dependence and trust in God is, ultimately, restored.

The whole worry of Paul for the church in Galatia is whether they can trust in God alone or whether they will return to their legalism, their reaching for Jesus and then overreaching for just a bit of the law on the side. This is reiterated in the final commands Paul gives the church—do not boast in anything except Christ and his death and resurrection.

Jesus sends the disciples out in pairs to do work that they were not necessarily sure they could manage. From the outset of this motivational speech, Jesus says, "Be warned, though, that I'm sending you out as lambs among wolves" (v. 3). Clearly, the task could prove too big and the environs too unfriendly. Yet, the text tells us, "The seventy-two returned joyously, saying, 'Lord, even the demons submit themselves to us in your name.'" They learn, in this, that Jesus can be trusted even when they don't yet see the plan or the purpose.

Prayer of Confession

Mighty and merciful God, like Naaman, you call us to obey even when we don't understand your plan. Like the psalmist, we know what it is to trust in ourselves and be disappointed. Like the early church, we want to shore up our credentials with extra credit instead of trusting in you alone. Like the disciples, we are amazed when you manage to work through us anyway. Forgive us, Lord. Teach us to trust in you and you alone. And use us, Lord, to your purpose and plan. Amen.

Sending Words (Based on Galatians 6:9-16)

Friends in Christ, let's not get tired of doing good.
We will work for the good of all whenever we have an opportunity.
Whoever wants to look good by human standards will compel you to outward marks of religion.
But as for me, God forbid that I should boast about anything except for the cross of our Lord Jesus Christ. The world has been crucified to me through him, and I have been crucified to the world.
Brothers and sisters, may the grace of our Lord Jesus Christ be with your spirit.
Amen.

July 14, 2019

Passages: Amos 7:7-17; Psalm 82; Colossians 1:1-14; Luke 10:25-37

Congregational Prayer

Between various petitions for the needs of the self, the church, the community, the nation, and the world, utilize an interspersed refrain from Psalm 82.

We ask you, Lord:
Give justice to the lowly and the orphan; maintain the right of the poor and the destitute! Rescue the lowly and the needy. Deliver them from the power of the wicked!

Call to Confession

Like the legal scholar who questions Jesus, "And who is my neighbor?" (Luke 10:29), we are also people who desire to prove we are right. Jesus's point, in this parable and throughout his ministry, is that we cannot be made right without the intervention of a Savior who will forgive our sin. Let us turn to God in prayer, confessing our fault and depending only on Christ's mercy.

Assurance of Pardon

Friends in Christ, hear the good news: Christ Jesus, himself, came to earth, lived among us, taught, healed, and befriended all who would accept him. He is the only one who has perfectly loved his neighbor as himself. By his death and resurrection, we are forgiven, made right with God and with our neighbor and free to follow his example of mercy as he commands, "Go and do likewise" (Luke 10:37).

Preaching Theme

I recently attended a local elementary school's kindergarten graduation. The diminutive cap-and-gowned graduates were a squirming, adorable contrast to the pomp and circumstance of the occasion. It was both endearing and strange to watch, particularly as one parent came in with a large helium balloon emblazoned with one word: "Done!" One certainly hopes the six-year-old in question has not, in fact, completed her educational journey! This experience was an immersion in a self-congratulatory culture in which all the participants get a ribbon. As adults, we live into self-congratulations when we wear busyness as a badge of honor, we assign ourselves "life awards" for getting out of bed in the morning, or we #humblebrag all over social media.

By contrast, the Apostle Paul doesn't allow congratulations to rest on the faithful church in Colossae. Instead, he offers thanksgiving *for* them *to* God. The love they have for one another? It comes from the Spirit. Their faith in Christ might equally be translated as Christ's faithfulness in you. Their love, their hope, the word of truth—all of this was given to them by God. For all of this, Paul does not say "Congratulations!" to the church in Colossae. Instead he says, "We always give thanks to God, the Father of our Lord Jesus Christ" (v. 3). Thankfulness is the heart of this text, a recognition that, as the old hymn says, "all that we have is thine alone, a trust, O Lord, from thee."

Secondary Preaching Themes

One need look no further than the parable of the good Samaritan for evidence that our self-congratulatory nature is not a recent development in human nature. The parable begins with the questions of a legal scholar who "wanted to prove that he was right" or, in other translations, "want[ed] to justify himself" (v. 29 NRSV). The priest and the Levite do something similar when they encounter the bruised and beaten man on the side of the road. How they must have congratulated themselves for staying unsullied, keeping themselves pure and "holy"! And, for all that, they missed the opportunity to participate in the work of mercy that God laid out before them.

In a church context that includes children's messages or that allows for a bit of creativity and interaction, it might be helpful to go through Paul's prayer for the Colossians in verses 9-12, assigning physical objects to each of the requests Paul makes on the people's behalf, adding them in a heaping pile of those good things God intends: knowledge of God's will (a how-to guide on something), producing fruit (a small fruit-bearing plant in a pot); growing (a tape measure); being strengthened (dumbbells); endure everything (a bad-weather camping kit); and so forth. The goal is to visually create an image of the abundance Paul is praying that God will provide to the Colossian believers.

Sending Words (Based on Colossians 1:10-13)

Friends, live lives that are worthy of the Lord and pleasing to him in every way: by producing fruit in every good work and growing in the knowledge of God; by being strengthened through his glorious might so that you endure everything and have patience; and by giving thanks with joy to the Father. For it is God who rescued us from the control of darkness and transferred us into the kingdom of the Son God loves.

July 21, 2019

Passages: Amos 8:1-12; Psalm 52; Colossians 1:15-28; Luke 10:38-42

Call to Worship (Based on Psalm 52:8-9)

I am like a green olive tree in God's house;
I trust in God's faithful love forever and always.
I will give thanks to you, God, forever, because you have acted.
In the presence of your faithful people, I will hope in your name because it's so good.

Responsive Prayer of Illumination

The prophet Amos reminds us that we are to long for the word of the Lord:
"The days are surely coming, says the LORD God, when I will send hunger and thirst on the land; neither a hunger for bread, nor a thirst for water, but of hearing the LORD's words."
Like your people Israel, we long to hear your word, O Lord.
Our Savior, Jesus Christ, commends Mary for sitting at his feet, listening to his words:
"Mary has chosen the better part. It won't be taken away from her."
Like your friend Mary, we long to hear your word, O Lord.

Preaching Theme

Abraham Kuyper—the Dutch pastor, journalist, and statesman—once famously stated, "There is not a square inch in the whole domain of our human existence over which Christ, who is sovereign over all, does not already cry, 'You are mine,'"[1] While attributed to Kuyper, this sentiment is also found in Paul's proclamation in this morning's text. God is in charge of it all!

This, then, has lasting implications for how we are to engage the world in Christ's name. First, we are not to be afraid. Verses 15-20 are, likely, the lyrics of an ancient hymn—a fight song, more like. We have nothing to fear if our God is in charge of the whole creation! This means we can boldly pursue vocations in science, in art, in government, in medicine believing that God goes before us and meets us in "every square inch."

Second, we are not to allow our worship and praise to rest on earthly things because "every good gift, every perfect gift, comes from above" (Jas 1:17). Our admiration for a beautiful creation belongs to the one who created. Our delight in meaningful work belongs to the one who made us. Our thankfulness for loving relationships belongs to the one who loves us.

Secondary Preaching Themes

The song of Colossians 1:15-20 was intended for congregational singing, which makes it a logical lead-in to what comes next: an exploration of the communal nature of faith. This is why Paul writes, "You need to remain well established and rooted in faith and not shift away from the hope given in the good news that you heard" (v. 23). God is calling you to grow deep roots and to live in community.

With regard to deep roots, we observe Mary's example of sitting at Jesus's feet. We hear Amos predicting the shriveled roots of those who have not been fed and watered by the word of God. We explore the contrast, in Psalm 52, between those who don't "make God their refuge. Instead, they trusted in their own great wealth. They sought refuge in it—to their own destruction!" (v. 7). Those people are uprooted but, in contrast, "I am like a green olive tree in God's house; I trust in God's faithful love forever and always" (v. 8).

An image of rootedness and community is the giant sequoia tree, which can be twenty-five feet in diameter and almost three hundred feet high. But rather than growing roots deep, they grow their roots wide, intertwined with all the roots of all the other trees. And this is what allows them to withstand storms and rains and winds.

Affirmation of Faith (Based on Colossians 1:12-18)

Give thanks with joy to the Father! God made it so you could take part in the inheritance, in light granted to God's holy people.
God rescued us from the control of darkness and transferred us into the kingdom of the Son he loves.
Christ is the image of the invisible God. The firstborn of all creation;
Because all things were created by him: both in the heavens and on the earth, the things that are visible and the things that are invisible. Whether they are thrones or powers, or rulers or authorities, all things were created through him and for him.
He existed before all things, and all things are held together in him.
He is the head of the body, the church, who is the beginning, the one who is firstborn from among the dead so that he might occupy the first place in everything.

"Crazy Love: The Search for Unquenchable"

Luke 10:38-42

Lia McIntosh

We live in a crazy world of reality TV shows with plenty of drama. Just take a look at *The Bachelor*, *The Real Housewives*, and *Love & Hip Hop* and you'll see "outrageous" at its best. We've experienced political seasons play out as a divisive and outlandish spectacle. We live amidst the reality of economic instability and religious volatility. Yet, there's *something deep inside all of us that desires another kind of crazy. It's a crazy love.* Our souls are thirsty for a love that's everlasting. And yet, reality shows, political parties, and public institutions alone cannot quench this thirst. We need something more.

Today's message is titled "Crazy Love: The Search for Unquenchable." Our scripture is from the Gospel according to Luke chapter 10 verses 38 to 42.

I have the privilege of being a mom to Isaac, who's twelve, Aaron, who's ten, and Alexis, who is six years old. They spend most of their summers playing baseball, basketball, and soccer. Whether on the field or in the backyard I always know that within twenty minutes of practicing in the summer heat someone will say, "I'm so thirsty!" And so the debate begins as we discuss what they should drink. My preference as their mother is always water. But of course they'd rather have Gatorade, which is filled with sugar and comes in dozens of kid-friendly flavors like glacier freeze, rain berry, and lemon lime.

What's your drink of choice? Coffee, tea, soda, sports drinks? I have to admit that I'm a coffee lover and Diet Coke (not Pepsi) has a place in my refrigerator.

Oh yes, and then there's water. Science tells us that water is not only thirst quenching but has many benefits for our bodies in general and vital organs in particular.

Water:

Prevents dehydration

Regulates body temperature

Carries nutrients and oxygen to the cells

Provides moisture to the skin and other tissues

Helps prevent constipation

Cushions joints

Helps strengthen muscles

Helps to curb your appetite

It contains no calories, fat, or cholesterol, and is low in sodium. Now that part sounds good! An average healthy adult needs to consume at least eight glasses of water each day, and even more during the summer heat. I bet we could all drink more water to quench our physical thirst.

(Note: Pass out bottles of water to the congregation.)

Likewise, there is a *spiritual thirst* inside each of us. In our humanness we try to quench this spiritual thirst by television, sports, politics, relationships, and even money.

How do you quench your spiritual thirst?

Francis Chan in his book *Crazy Love* quotes John Piper from the book *God Is the Gospel,* and asks about spiritual thirst in this way:

> If you could have heaven, with no sickness, and with all the friends you've ever had on earth, and all the food you ever liked, and all the leisure activities, and all the natural beauties you ever saw, all the physical pleasures you ever tasted, and no human conflict or any natural disaster, could you be satisfied with heaven, if Christ was not there?[2]

Would you take all the pleasures of life without Jesus? Would you take it?

This seems like an easy question to ask in church, but if we're honest, it's a tough question to answer in our humanness. Just like we know that water is the best beverage for us, but don't drink it like we should, we are also tempted to take all the pleasures of the world and leave Jesus behind.

Here's why. Most of us have tasted the world and everything it has to offer, but we have failed to nourish ourselves with the fullness of the love of Jesus, so we settle for substitutes.

- We pray and ask God to pay our bills because we have not tasted the fullness of an abundant God who can lead us toward generosity.

- We pray and ask God to fix our bad relationships because we have not tasted the fullness of God's love that is immeasurably more satisfying than what we as humans can give to one another.

- We pray and ask God to take our physical ailments away because we've learned we settle for a body fixing when what God really desires is a heart fixing that will last forever even as our bodies age.

We've tasted the world and everything it has to offer, and often Jesus seems so far away. We are distracted and settling for substitutes just like soda, Gatorade, and coffee instead of living water.

In our scripture today we encounter this predicament as two sisters, Martha and Mary, are anticipating a knock on their door. They have heard that Jesus is on the way. Mary and Martha are excited about Jesus's coming. They've experienced his miracles, his magnificence. They are like family to one another. Yet, Martha and Mary each respond in different ways when Jesus arrives. Martha immediately goes into action, ensuring the house and food are suitable for Jesus. Martha's gift of hospitality necessitates a special meal, fresh water, and the table being set. I envision, Mary has butterflies in her stomach and is so excited that all she can do is look out the window and anticipate Jesus's arrival.

Are you more like Martha or Mary? (Take a poll by show of hands.)

The story continues when Jesus arrives and Mary sits at Jesus's feet and listens. Yet, in verse 40 Martha is distracted with all the preparations. I wonder if Martha is anxious and troubled about more than the meal. Martha may have had some bills that needed to be paid, a relationship that was troubled, or even health issues that are unresolved. We, like Martha, understand what it's like to be in the presence of Jesus and still be distracted.

So picture this…

Martha is walking around Jesus. Mary is sitting at Jesus's feet.

Martha is fatigued. Mary is nourished.

Martha is consumed by the work of her hands. Mary is centered on the needs of her heart.

Can you picture yourself there in that room with Jesus? I can. I am often Martha, meaning well but focusing on all the things that need to be accomplished "for" Jesus rather than on the joy of being *with* Jesus. Maybe you know what that's like.

Like Mary, our deepest thirst is for relationship rather than routine. We need the presence of God beyond the posture of religious righteousness and cultured congeniality.

Yet, in a world full of substitutes how do we quench our essential thirst?

First, sit at Jesus's feet and have a drink. In this time of biblical history, culturally it was unsuitable for a woman to sit at the feet of a rabbi, a male teacher. Mary's radical act of love is certainly not out of obligation, but out of adoration. She risks social shame for the sake of quenching her essential thirst. She longs to be with God above all else.

How will you make room for Jesus in your life not out of obligation, but out of outpouring love? When will you stop, rest, and bask in God's presence in prayer, study, worship, and silence? How will you eliminate distractions and singularly drink from the well of living water at least once a day?

Take a moment and write down one action you can begin to take this week.

A second way we quench our essential thirst is:

Invite others to drink with us. Like Martha, I grew up learning the value of hospitality. We often had friends and family drop by to visit, especially on Sundays. I remember our big party of the year was on New Year's Day! Dozens of people visited to eat dinner, watch football games, and enjoy deep belly laughs of joy. Our family shopped, cooked, and cleaned for days in advance. But, moments before the first guests arrived my mother would change into her party dress, put on her favorite music, and prepare to enjoy the fun. Never mind that some closets never got cleaned and shoes were stuffed underneath the bed. Welcoming people into our homes and lives is a gift worth sharing. Communities of grace are a place to quench our essential thirst. Whether it happens over a meal in homes, with coffee at the local café, or in the church fellowship hall, true hospitality makes people feel seen, heard, and valued. That's living water.

I envision Jesus flipping the proverbial "water bottle" and saying, "Drink from my well of living water first and then share my love with others."

Ahhh... that's crazy love.

Let us pray.

Prayer: God, help us to open ourselves up to you. We confess that we've tried to impress you and others with our works. We have been in the kitchen distracted. God, we need to come to your table and drink from your fountain of everlasting love. For those of us who need a drink of your living water for the first time, Lord in your mercy, hear our prayer. For those of us who have been at the table but have been too distracted to bask in your presence, help us to come back to you. Lord in your mercy, forgive us. For those of us who have been too busy to share your love with others, help us to strip away our distractions and make room for the new relationships you put in our path. Be, O Lord, our eternal love and thirst quencher.

Amen.

July 28, 2019

Passages: Hosea 1:2-10; Psalm 85; Colossians 2:6-15, (16-19); Luke 11:1-13

Prayer of Confession (Based on Psalm 85)

Lord, you've forgiven your people's wrongdoing; you've covered all their sins.
You, the God who can save us, restore us!
Won't you bring us back to life again so that your people can rejoice in you?
Show us your faithful love, Lord! Give us your salvation!
Let me hear what the Lord God says, because he speaks peace to his people and to his faithful ones. Don't let them return to foolish ways.
Righteousness walks before God, making a road for his steps.

Assurance of Pardon (Based on Colossians 2:13-14)

Friends in Christ, hear the good news:
When you were dead because of the things you had done wrong, God made you alive with Christ and forgave all the things you had done wrong. He destroyed the record of the debt we owed, with its requirements that worked against us. He canceled it by nailing it to the cross. Thanks be to God, we are forgiven in Christ Jesus our Lord.

Preaching Theme

In acting classes you might learn the term *upstaging*, in which one character's actions are so out-of-sync with everything else happening on stage that the audience turns their attention to that person. This is helpful when intentional, but it is distracting when a minor actor accidentally "upstages" the main action.

In Colossians 2 we see a battle between philosophy, foolish deception, and human traditions in which each is working to upstage the other. Each gets louder and more demanding until, in a trade center like Colossae, you couldn't go anywhere without someone trying to sell you something. The marketplace was filled with noises, newness, intrigue. It was easy for the people of God to get sucked in by the barkers and the hawkers.

When beginning actors are given the task to "upstage" one another, they inevitably get louder, flashier, stranger until there is cacophony on stage. At that point, an experienced actor knows that the only way to upstage is to be quiet, to be calm, to be deliberate. This behavior is so out-of-sync with the rest of the stage that the audience can't help but pay attention.

In a similar fashion, Christ entered a cacophonous world and drew attention not by shouting louder but by being present, not by trying to advantage himself to the detriment of others, not by being flashy but by giving freely of himself, all the way to death. In this, we are told, "He exposed [the rulers and authorities] to public disgrace by leading them in a triumphal parade."

Secondary Preaching Themes

The strange story of Hosea is one of God's choice to "upstage" guilt with mercy, infidelity with faithfulness. "Go, marry a prostitute and have children of prostitution, for the people of the land commit great prostitution by deserting the LORD. . . . Yet the number of the people of Israel will be like the sand of the sea, which can be neither measured nor numbered; and in the place where it was said to them, 'You are not my people,' it will be said to them, 'Children of the living God'" (vv. 2, 10).

Similarly, the psalmist is caught in a tension between God's anger and God's love. Both are fighting for attention on stage, which in this psalm is creation. The curse of God's anger affects the whole world but, likewise, the blessing of God's love counteracts, upstages, the harmful effects of the curse. As the beloved Christmas carol tells it, "He comes to make his blessings flow, far as the curse is found."[3] God's love will upstage it all in the end!

Congregational Prayer (Based on Luke 11:2-4)

Father, hallowed be your name (offer praises of God's name and character).
Your kingdom come (offer prayers for peace and justice among the kingdoms of this earth).
Give us each day our daily bread (offer prayers for national and local organizations that work to alleviate homelessness, hunger, and poverty).
Forgive us our sins, for we also forgive everyone who sins against us (pray for reconciliation within the body of Christ and our families).
And lead us not into temptation (offer prayers for all present, the sins and addictions that hinder us).
For thine is the kingdom and the power and the glory forever. Amen.

Sending Words (Based on Colossians 2:6-7)

Friends, live in Christ Jesus the Lord in the same way as you received him. Be rooted and built up in him, be established in faith, and overflow with thanksgiving just as you were taught.

August 4, 2019

Passages: Hosea 11:1-11; Psalm 107:1-9, 43; Colossians 3:1-11; Luke 12:13-21

Call to Worship (Based on Psalm 107)

Give thanks to the Lord because he is good!
His faithful love lasts forever!
God redeemed us from the power of our enemies
God gathered us from various countries, from east and west, north and south
God satisfies us when we are thirsty and fills us with good things when we are hungry!
Let us thank the Lord for his faithful love and his wondrous works for all people!

Preaching Theme

When my legs grew too long to ride my tricycle, my parents bought me a bicycle, or as my fellow elementary school classmates called it—a "two-wheeler." Only it was really a "four-wheeler" because there were two little wheels attached at the rear tire. I rode my two-wheeler up and down the sidewalk in front of my family's home until I was accustomed to riding upright.

One day, my father removed the training wheels so that I could ride without them. I fell a few times before my father jogged alongside me, holding the seat to keep me balanced. After a few laps, riding my two-wheeler became a little easier. When I made a U-turn at the end of the imaginary finish line, I was shocked to see my father at the other end, watching me with his arms folded and a proud grin on his face. I was so focused on avoiding another fall, I had no idea how long I had been pedaling without him. But I did it! I was one of the big kids! I could ride a bike all by myself, without training wheels or my father's assistance.

Once I achieved this new sense of independence, any memory of my little red tricycle, the number of times I fell, or my father's help vanished. It was as though I did it all on my own, but that is not the truth.

When the children of Israel wandered through the wilderness, God cared for them, raised them the way a loving father raises his child. After his own presence in their lives, the greatest gift their heavenly Father gave to Israel was their freedom from their slavery to the Egyptians. But when Israel was liberated and empowered to build new lives for themselves, they forgot the one who fed them, kept them safe, healed them, and led them into their new life. So much so that they preferred instant gratification and the profits from injustice to the longsuffering, patient God who gave them new life.

Although Israel's disobedience provoked great anger in the Lord, to the point where he is ready to destroy his living creation, his overtaking compassion prevents him from bringing destruction. Like any good father, the Lord will still chastise his children. Yet he is always ready to joyfully welcome us into his good graces when we run to him asking forgiveness, ready to conform to his image, and filled with gratitude.

Secondary Preaching Themes (Luke 12:13-21; Colossians 3:1-11)

Jesus shares a parable about a rich fool, warning against greed and being self-centered. The relentless pursuit of material possessions is a powerful distraction from growing an intimate relationship with Jesus. When we become self-absorbed, we neglect to pray, study God's word, and prepare for Jesus's return. Nothing that may be accumulated on earth is as valuable as the eternal riches we have in God's kingdom.

The Apostle Paul reminds us that "Christ is our life" (Col 3:4). When we become followers of Jesus Christ, our nature is renewed. We become hidden in the risen Christ in that our values and lifestyles are aligned with his teachings and nature. As we conform with Christ, our behavior changes. Over time, our lives are no longer in step with that of popular culture, but in obedience to God. Submission to the way of the Lord places us in his favor, out of the way of his wrath.

Prayer of Repentance

Gracious and loving God, we thank you for who you are in our lives. Too often, in our pursuit of a better life, in our allowing ourselves to be distracted by life's challenges, we forget that we belong to you. We forget that we are hidden in you with Christ. Please forgive us for allowing sin to overtake us. Remind us, forever your children, to draw closer to you, intimately and deeper still. In the name of our Lord and Savior, Jesus Christ, we pray. Amen.

Sending Forth

Go with us, Lord, as we leave this place. We invite your Holy Spirit and word to continue to minister to us throughout the week until we gather together again to worship you. When we hear you whisper our names, we will not ignore your voice. When you correct us, we will learn and obey. As you express your love toward us, we will adore you with overflowing gratitude. In the name of our true Lord and Savior, Jesus Christ, we pray. Amen.

August 11, 2019

Passages: *Isaiah 1:1, 10-20; Psalm 50:1-8, 22-23; Hebrews 11:1-3, 8-16; Luke 12:32-40*

Gathering Prayer

Gracious and compassionate God, we are grateful for your presence. We remember that you are God. You are our God. We know that you are speaking and we humbly gather at your feet to hear every word. We invite you to remove every distraction, open our spiritual ears, and increase our understanding so that we are empowered to live into what you share with us today. Know, Lord God, that we love you. In the name of Jesus Christ we pray. Amen.

Preaching Theme

I once heard of a church that celebrated Holy Communion during the first Sunday of the month. After the pastor delivered a preaching series on this sacrament, the leadership of the church was so moved, that they asked the pastor if we could celebrate Holy Communion every week. The pastor joyfully agreed.

After several months of this weekly celebration, the pastor announced that we would return to a monthly celebration. Over these several months, the pastor discovered that congregants treated the Lord's Supper as a "free pass to sin." The people of the church behaved in ways that were antithetical to Jesus's teachings all week, then participated in Holy Communion so that they could start misbehaving again with a clean slate.

When God spoke through the prophet Isaiah, he expressed his anger toward the people of Judah for having similar attitudes toward sacred rituals meant to honor and worship him. In Isaiah 1:13, the Lord exclaims, "I can't stand wickedness with celebration!"

Christ followers are called to be "all in." It is an affront before the Most High to treat our dedicated worship time like an item on our to-do lists to be checked off. Our lives are to be dedicated to demonstrating Christ's love by being just, protecting the helpless, and showing kindness to all. Observing the sacraments means nothing to God when our hearts are cold and we live in habitual disobedience to God's word and nature.

God's anger is temporary, tempered with compassion, yet unavoidable when we are disobedient. When we sincerely, humbly return to God and his ways, seeking forgiveness, his arms are always open to receive us; his heart is always open to hear our prayers.

Prayer of Confession and Repentance

Dear Heavenly Master, we bow down before you with broken hearts. We confess that we have taken you for granted. We confess that we have allowed the distractions of life, our own selfishness to diminish sincere worship. Our hearts have been far from you when we celebrate the sacraments. We have not allowed you to transform our lives so that they are pleasing in your sight. With humility we repent of these sins against you and ask for your forgiveness. We submit ourselves to you totally and completely. We are all in from this moment on. All glory and honor be unto you, our God! In Jesus's wonderful name we pray. Amen.

Secondary Preaching Themes (Psalm 50:1-8, 22-23; Luke 12:32-40)

God still speaks. In the book of Genesis, God spoke order over the earth and the creation of the universe. God spoke to the prophet Jeremiah calling him into ministry. In Psalm 50, God speaks a word of judgment over a rebellious Israel. Our Lord is not one to be forgotten. He expects and deserves faithfulness from his children. Yet no matter how angry he becomes, he always lets us know what will restore us to his favor, avoiding punishment. God is worthy of honor, gratitude, and praise. The Lord is pleased with his people when we make the sincerest sacrifice: thanksgiving.

Devotion to God means being mindful of his presence every day. It means being engaged in an ever-deepening relationship with Jesus Christ, learning to trust him with our very lives. When out of love we choose to treat the Lord as a loving parent, friend, and sovereign, we will obey his commands, faithfully serving him. Our hearts and lives will then be prepared when Jesus returns. Being mindful of this fact will further motivate us to live as though Christ is returning today.

Benediction

"Faith is the reality of what we hope for, the proof of what we don't see. By faith we understand that the universe has been created by a word from God so that the visible came into existence from the invisible." We leave this place a forgiven people, renewed by the love of God and made righteous by the blood of Jesus. We go into the world as a people of faith, living into a new reality where we see God's creative movement in each other and our surroundings. Our lives will be a blessing to God. Thank you, God, for blessing us today. In your Son's name we pray. Amen.

August 18, 2019

*Passages: Isaiah 5:1-7; Psalm 80:1-2, 8-19; Hebrews 11:29–12:2;
Luke 12:49-56*

Gathering Prayer

God of all creation, you are welcome in this place, in our hearts, in our lives. Let our worship be pleasing in your sight. Let every note we sing be sweet sounds in your ears. Knit our heartstrings together with yours so that we are always practicing your presence. Our entire being is focused on you. Receive us, O God, with open arms. Receive our adoration. In the name of our true Lord and Savior we pray. Amen.

Preaching Theme

By faith are two powerful words. They defy the impossible when we practice them. The writer of the book of Hebrews reminds us of the mind-boggling feats performed by God's power when helpless people chose to believe in him in spite of the peril in which they found themselves.

Unforeseen crises, natural disasters, and other disruptive events may cause Christians to ask, "Where is God in all this?" Meditating on the reminiscences of Hebrews may change the question to "Where is my faith in God in all this?" What is clear among all the examples provided in this passage is that the heroes and heroines in the text had personal experiences with the God of Israel who gave them victories. Their personal interactions, the testimonies they heard, acts of God that they witnessed gave them the kind of faith that honored God so much, that God was honored to do the impossible for them and their people.

Faith is built by knowing God through Jesus Christ. Just as we get to know people through mundane interactions, we may also get to know our Lord. Authentic conversation in and outside the context of prayer brings a closeness to the heart of God that increases our faith. The Holy Spirit will illuminate scripture in a way that not only will we understand it, but our eyes will be open to see its truth in action in the world. We will see the evidence that God's promises are trustworthy. When impossible situations emerge—and they often do—even in our worry, we can stand on what we have learned of and from God, calling on him to give us peace while he works out the problem for our good. By faith, we will trust the Most High for the outcome, knowing that God always acts out of love when we honor God in this way.

At times, we grow weary. If we remind ourselves of what God has already done for us, recognizing what he is already doing for us, God will revive our faith, giving us the second wind we need to keep running by faith.

Responsive Reading (Based on Psalm 80)

Please come back, God of heavenly forces! Look down from heaven and perceive it!
Attend to this vine, this root that you planted with your strong hand.
Let your hand be with the one on your right side—with the one whom you secured as your own.
Then we will not turn away from you!
Revive us so that we can call on your name. Restore us, Lord God of heavenly forces! Make your face shine so that we can be saved!

Secondary Preaching Themes (Isaiah 5:1-7; Luke 12:49-56)

In this Isaiah passage, the Lord is the loving gardener who planted and cared for a vineyard. He provided everything the vines needed to flourish, to bear healthy wine grapes. In spite of the extravagant provision of care, the vines strangely bore rotten grapes. This is how the gardener describes the people of Israel.

God blessed them with loving care, making them a numerous people empowered for generations of prosperity. They forgot and ultimately turned against their heavenly benefactor. Because of this God will remove the protection they once enjoyed so that they will be reminded of the good they once enjoyed through the generosity of the Lord.

Such punishment will be avoided when we choose not to be distracted by personal gain, but to remember who God is in our lives, while living to please him.

Many of the values that are upheld by twenty-first-century society are similar to those during the age of the Roman Empire. Striving for power and material possessions at the expense of the poor and the weak is still very common today. Living into the teachings of Jesus—living moral lives when it seems that is not profitable; considering others above ourselves; creating systems that protect and empower the helpless—are strange concepts to many people. Living according to Christ's teachings is what God requires of us, in spite of the fact that we will find ourselves in conflict with those who do not agree with our lifestyle choices.

Closing Congregational Prayer

Dear wonderful Lord, we thank you for our time together. Let us see you every day, remembering your love and power in action in the world and in us. In the name of Jesus Christ we pray. Amen.

August 25, 2019

Passages: Jeremiah 1:4-10; Psalm 71:1-6; Hebrews 12:18-29; Luke 13:10-17

Call to Worship (Psalm 71)

*I've taken refuge in you, L*ORD*.*
    Don't let me ever be put to shame!
Deliver me and rescue me by your righteousness!
    Bend your ear toward me and save me!
Be my rock of refuge
    where I can always escape.
You commanded that my life be saved
    because you are my rock and my fortress.
My God, rescue me from the power of the wicked;
    rescue me from the grip of the wrongdoer and the oppressor
    *because you are my hope, L*ORD*.*
    *You, L*ORD*, are the one I've trusted since childhood.*
I've depended on you from birth—
. . .
    my praise is always about you.

Preaching Theme

Everyone who follows Jesus Christ is called to serve in order to advance God's kingdom here on earth. For some, that is an intimidating prospect. This is largely due to folks who limit serving in ministry to preaching in a pulpit or serving as a chaplain. Ministry is serving in many ways that do not include public speaking or comforting persons who are enduring physical illness. Serving Jesus Christ in whatever capacity he chooses for us requires willingness, trust, and obedience. The Lord will guide us into whatever additional formal training is needed, if any at all.

We see this in God's calling Jeremiah to become a prophet. In his case, Jeremiah was indeed called to a public-speaking ministry, a dangerous one at that. What is most intriguing about this call, however, is that when Jeremiah received the calling, he was in his late teens to early twenties. He really had not been alive long enough to develop any great oratory skills. Quite naturally, he was also afraid of how he would be received if he accepted the call.

How gracious of God to engage young Jeremiah in a conversation. Jeremiah understood that in this vision he was voicing his own objections to the God of Israel that he had already heard about through testimonies. Without this intimate dialogue, it would be difficult to imagine that Jeremiah would be willing to dedicate his life to doing something so far outside his comfort zone, sacrificing any possibility of getting married and having a family as was common in his culture. Yet this interaction in the presence of God, though difficult, was probably strangely peaceful and comforting.

However God calls us to serve, we should trust the Lord well enough to respectfully voice our concerns or objections to him, even if not calmly. We should also understand that however unqualified we may think we are, God knew our pedigrees before he decided to call us into service. God also knew what our objections would be and how our personalities would get in the way of the work God needs us to do. Yet God calls us because God knows that we will be willing, faithful, and obedient. God calls us into partnership with him based on the strengths God has already given us and the new strength that is on the way.

Congregational Prayer

Lord of heaven and earth, we are grateful for intimate conversations with you! It is a great and wonderful day when we can share our hearts with you, knowing that you will hear us without judgment. When you speak, we will hear. Joyfully we will serve you in divine partnership with you. Call us, send us, we will go. In Jesus's name we pray. Amen.

Secondary Preaching Themes (Luke 13:10-17; Hebrews 12:18-29)

Once again, Jesus ticked off one of the leaders of the synagogue. Going about his Father's business by serving faithfully was central to the Savior's lifestyle. Sometimes this required a doctrinal violation. In this case, during the Sabbath Jesus healed a woman who had been disabled by a spirit.

Faithful service to the Lord may sometimes necessitate an act of obedience in inconvenient settings in the presence of persons who will not understand what and why we are doing what God commanded us to do. We must do it anyway. Our service to God is much greater than the rules set by humankind. We are to comply out of respect for authority, but when the greater good is to be accomplished for God and his people, God's bigger picture must come first.

The writer of the book of Hebrews warns: "See to it that you don't resist the one who is speaking" (Heb 12:25). The one who is speaking is God. God is judging, teaching, instructing, commanding, celebrating on earth and in heaven. God rules an unshakeable kingdom that he has waiting for his faithful servants. We are to serve

God with gratitude, expecting the benefits of his partnership as well as the gift of citizenship in heavenly places.

Sending Forth

God is moving in the world and calls us to be his vessels. Let us trust that God is with us, enjoying the time we spend with God. Let us serve God with joyful hearts and the expectation that God will do the impossible through us in small and big ways. Let us look past our inadequacies and see the power of God. Let us go, being and making disciples of Jesus Christ for the kingdom of God!

September 1, 2019

Passages: Jeremiah 2:4-13; Psalm 81:1, 10-16; Hebrews 13:1-8, 15-16;
Luke 14:1, 7-14

Call to Worship

Sing for joy to God our strength; shout aloud to the God of Jacob!
Begin the music, strike the timbrel, play the melodious harp and lyre.
Open wide your mouths and hearts that the Lord may fill you with good things!
The Lord will feed us with the finest wheat and satisfy us with honey from the rock.

Preaching Theme

The folks at the Revised Common Lectionary are not fooling us by coyly suggesting we skip over five verses in Luke 14. As when a parent forbids a child to look at a certain chapter in a book on the living room shelf, so we just have to take a peek to see what is in those forbidden verses. We need the full context here.

Luke 14:1 tells us that Jesus had been invited for a dinner party at the house of a "prominent Pharisee." But why was Jesus invited? He was not a real popular person among the Pharisees, after all. Based on the text I suspect he was not invited out of love. In fact, it looks like they were setting Jesus up. As such, it is neither accidental nor coincidental that Jesus immediately encounters a man with dropsy. Dropsy was what today we would call edema, which likely meant his breathing was labored, and also his face, legs, feet, and hands were swollen because of a cardio-pulmonary problem that caused fluid to build up throughout his body. Likely he looked pathetic.

As his devious hosts suspected, Jesus cannot resist the urge to help. "Would it be all right by you if I healed this man? Is that a lawful thing to do on the Sabbath?"

Silence.

The dinner party is off to a really rocky start! But it gets worse when in reaction to people's jockeying for the more important seats at the dining table Jesus begins to urge a bit of humility rather than brashly trying to get the best seat in the house. Did the people blush? Probably. But Jesus is not done. He has more to say and it is not what you'd call Emily Post etiquette to say what Jesus does at this party. Ultimately he tells a parable that was a direct rebuke to his own host for not caring more about the last, least, lost, and lonely of the world the way God wants us to.

– 97

Luke doesn't tell us how that Sabbath-day dinner party ended. But you have the feeling that when Jesus left, his host did not smile and say, "Come again!" When next we see Jesus at a dinner in the next chapter, it will be in the company of "sinners" with the Pharisees on the outside looking in, sneering at Jesus in judgment. They didn't get it. Not ever. We know who Jesus's kind of people were. The question to ask of ourselves and of our congregations in a sermon on Luke 14 is whether Jesus's kind of people are our kind of people.

Secondary Preaching Theme

The writer Dallas Willard notes in his fine book *The Divine Conspiracy* that we often forget what the goal of discipleship is: we really are supposed to live like Jesus.[1] To become Jesus. To be generous and sacrificial like Jesus. This is not a metaphor. This is not some overblown aspiration. This really is to be the bright center of our lives. And it may involve suffering. It may involve real sacrifice of various kinds. But, of course, there is always a danger lurking here, too, and it can be seen somewhat in this list of what some Bibles call "Concluding Exhortations" in Hebrews 13. The danger is turning these attempts to live like Jesus into something that does an end-run on Jesus's sacrifice by tempting us to think that it is our obedience that gets us rewarded with a free trip to heaven by and by.

We should not preach that message, but people like it when we do. To paraphrase an observation I once heard William Willimon make during a seminar, people will thank the preacher for this. "Thank you, Pastor! Thank you for telling me what to *do* to make sure God will love me again this week." But as a colleague of mine says, that undercuts grace. We ought not to preach "shouldy sermons." Because when we go to Jesus "outside the city" as Hebrews 13 commends, one of the first things we notice is that Jesus did what we never could: his perfect sacrifice alone is what saves us. It's all grace. It's not about us. Given the enormity of Jesus's saving grace, everything we do to be like Jesus is just one giant and extended way to say "Thank you!" And that is what Hebrews 13 commends indeed.

Parting Words (from Hebrews 13)

Go forth in the love of the Lord your God. Be friendly, welcome strangers, always be open to the presence of the angels themselves hidden in your midst. And remember in all things, the Lord is your helper—do not be afraid!

September 8, 2019

Passages: Jeremiah 18:1-11; Psalm 139:1-6, 13-18; Philemon 1-21;
Luke 14:25-33

Prayer of Confession (Based on Psalm 139)

O Lord, you have examined me and know me inside and out. You see what I do right but you see also all that I do wrong. You know me better than I know myself. You see sins I have actually forgotten that I committed. Forgive me, dear God. You who have seen me in the womb even before another person on earth could see me. Please see me now again as penitent, as truly sorry for my sin. On your grace, dear God, I rest my plea. For Jesus's sake, Amen.

Preaching Theme

Large congregations may or may not be an indicator of faithfulness to the gospel, but in many places, big crowds equal big success. But if the Gospels make one thing clear, it is that Jesus never regarded a large following as necessarily a good sign. In fact, he seemed intent on a regular basis to thin out the crowds that followed him. The closing verses of Luke 14 are a classic example. Notice how Luke structures the narrative. We are told in verse 25 that "large crowds were traveling with Jesus" only to have Jesus immediately turn to that same throng of people to say some things that seemed calculated to turn people off. The call to hate father, mother, spouse, and children is a tad on the harsh side and surely did not fail to make at least a few folks—and perhaps more than a few folks—turn away.

That was curious enough. But Jesus then goes on to tell two quasi-parables (they are really more like analogies) that talk about counting the cost and doing prudent calculations in advance of undertaking major projects. The upshot of these two analogies is easy enough to discern. But the way Jesus told them seems to be a left-handed rebuke to the crowd. It's almost as though Jesus is chiding the many people who were following him for not having a clue as to what they were doing.

For those of us who preach, this passage has a lot of relevance. After all, how many of us in the church today are there in large part because we were raised in the church? Yes, at some point most of us made some kind of conscious decision to be a follower of Jesus: we willingly went through confirmation, we initiated our own profession of faith, we underwent the sacrament of baptism, and so on. But do those formal, "typical" ways of growing up into church membership rise to the level of thoughtful seriousness and astute calculations that Jesus talks about in Luke 14? In short, do we find it altogether too easy to fall into line behind Jesus?

Secondary Preaching Theme

Abraham Lincoln's Gettysburg Address is noteworthy because it made a huge historical impact but did so through a speech consisting of a scant 272 words. Paul's letter to Philemon is like that. It's far and away Paul's shortest letter—it's more of a memo, just 334 words in the original Greek. But it packed a punch. It also presents a kind of master class in the art of subtlety. Paul does not order Philemon to be kind to—and finally to release from slavery—the runaway slave Onesimus. But he musters a lot of gospel rhetoric to tell Philemon to do this anyway.

Paul wants the gospel to take hold in Philemon's life and to sink down roots. So in verses 8 and 9 Paul does not command Philemon to treat Onesimus like a brother instead of a slave, but rather Paul cajoles—he sidles up alongside Philemon to help him see the sweet gospel reasonableness of adopting a new viewpoint. Paul then continues, laying it on pretty thick. He calls Onesimus "my very heart." Then note the quick shift in rhetoric in verse 16: first Paul suggests that Philemon receive Onesimus back not as a slave but as a brother. But before that same verse is finished Paul switches from the *suggestion* that Onesimus be seen as a brother to the absolute statement that when Onesimus returns to Philemon, he *will be* a brother in the Lord!

And just in case Philemon thinks he maybe could get away with *not* following through on Paul's advice, Paul rounds things out in verse 22 by saying, "Oh yes, and one more thing: I will visit you soon so get a room ready." It was Paul's none-too-subtle way of saying, "If you ignore my advice, I will find out soon enough."

The radical trajectory of the gospel and its reshaping of all human relationships is seldom on better display than in this brief but powerful memo from Paul to Philemon!

Parting Blessing (from Psalm 139)

Wherever you go, the Lord goes with you. When you work and when you rest, when you travel and when you arrive, when you prepare to speak and after you have spoken, the Lord is with you. May the Lord bless you and keep you in all your ways and accompany you with his grace and favor always. Amen.

September 15, 2019

Passages: Jeremiah 4:11-12, 22-28; Psalm 14; 1 Timothy 1:12-17; Luke 15:1-10

Call to Worship (from Psalm 14)

Fools say in their hearts, "There is no God!"
But we declare the truth: the Lord our God is the true God of the cosmos!
The Lord our God has saved us by his grace!
Therefore we celebrate, we rejoice, we worship our one true God now and always!

Preaching Theme

As Luke frames the parable, there are two audiences: the Pharisees who are out on the fringes, sneering at Jesus for the bad company he was keeping at table and the "sinners," the "bad company" with whom Jesus was sitting. Verse 3 informs us that Jesus "told them this parable," but the antecedent used for "them" is not clear: Is it the "tax collectors and sinners" or the eye-rolling and snippy Pharisees? Well, it is probably both, and yet it is instructive to wonder how differently these parables sounded in the ears of those two groups.

Let's start with the "bad company." To them these must have been great stories, because if they needed a reminder that they were the ones God needed to seek out and find, all they had to do was look over their shoulders at the scolding religious leaders. The Pharisees never failed to signal the message that folks like these "sinners" were not God's kind of people. They were lost to God. So if you fit into the category of a "lost cause" but then heard Jesus tell three stories about how God is the champion of the lost . . . well, it must have sounded like good news for sure.

It goes without saying that Jesus's parables sounded rather different in the ears of the Pharisees. In the parable of the lost sheep and the parable of the lost coin, joy busts out all over and there is no mistaking the fact that such divine joy is getting aimed at Jesus's "bad company" and not at the Pharisees. But in the end—just to be sure no one misses the point—Jesus will conclude with an elder brother refusing to enter into the joy of a party, and there is no way the Pharisees missed recognizing themselves in the portrait of that surly kid.

I wonder sometimes which set of ears most characterizes many people in the church yet today. Does the gospel sound wonderful to us only when we see ourselves as the target of God's grace and joy and happiness? Or does it sound best to us when we see others getting caught up in the divine embrace, even if those "others" are people very unlike us? And if we can feel joy over the salvation of "others," is it because we properly know that when you get right down to it, we are all the same? If we stop thinking in terms of "us versus them" in the church, maybe we will arrive at a day when we all have just one set of ears through which to hear parables like the ones in Luke 15: ears that are highly adept at picking out the tune of sheer joy that is the gospel of our Lord Jesus Christ!

Secondary Preaching Theme

In her classic ecological book *Silent Spring*, author Rachel Carson feared that the day would come when springtime would be silent because no birds would be alive to warble their beautiful tunes, no loons would cruise atop lakes to issue their hauntingly lovely cry: spring would be silent because pollution would have wiped out these creatures, obliterating them into extinction.[2]

"Silent Spring" could be an apt title for Jeremiah 4. It's difficult to discern if the destruction of the earth is a result of the creation's reacting to the evil of the Israelites or whether God is the one actively destroying the land. Or maybe it's both. But the instructive point is that there is a clear link between human sin and the ruination of the non-human parts of creation. Whether the natural fallout of human abuse of nature or some more direct result of God's anger at such evil, the fact is that the whole creation suffers when God's people repeatedly fail to follow God's ways.

In fact, in Jeremiah 4:23 we get a picture of un-creation, of chaos, as Jeremiah uses words that echo directly the "formless and empty" nature of the universe in Genesis 1:1 before God began to impose the order of his creation on the world. Sin, in other words, unmakes God's works. It shakes what should be rock-solid (mountains and hills) and makes the earth uninhabitable for people and birds and flocks and herds alike.

Everything gets ruined but...that is not the end of the story. Evil and the sullying of creation do not get the last word; only the creator God Yahweh does, and his last word is a return to life, to flourishing, to hope. But in the meantime, all creation groans (as the Apostle Paul put it some centuries after Jeremiah's time) under the weight of sin.

Doxology (from 1 Timothy 1)

Now to the king of the ages, to the immortal, invisible, and only God, may honor and glory be given to him forever and always! Amen.

September 22, 2017

Passages: Jeremiah 8:18–9:1; Psalm 79:1-9; 1 Timothy 2:1-7;
Luke 16:1-13

Prayer of Confession (from Psalm 79)

*Dear God, we know we have sinned against you. And we know that in your holiness you
cannot ignore our sins or brush them away lightly. But in your great compassion, cover
our sins. Come to us and do not delay to apply to us again the healing balm of your grace
and mercy. Deliver us and save us for the sake of your name. This we pray in the name of
Jesus, our Savior, Amen.*

Preaching Theme

Luke 16:1-13 is the oddest parable. The parable's hero is anything but: he's a
crook, a swindler, a cheat. To save his own skin once he realizes he is on the verge of
being fired, a certain shrewd manager goes behind his boss's back, cooks the books so
as to curry favor among many people, and so in this way feathers his future nest for
after he loses his job.

Startlingly, when the boss gets wind of these shenanigans, he is not angry! He
approves. He claps the manager on the shoulder and says in essence, "You've done
well for yourself!" So what's the point here? Well, not what you expect. Jesus finishes
the parable and then says to the disciples, "And you know what? There's something to
all that! The children of light could learn a thing or two from this scoundrel." Really?

What is it about the shrewd manager's attitude that Jesus finds useful? Perhaps
this: he gave thought to the future and it shaped his actions in the present. Further, he
knew that for now monetary resources are one way to secure the kind of future vision
you have drawn for yourself. So even though in his case it meant being devious, his
desperate desire to see his future materialize helped him conclude that it would be
worth it to take the risks he did.

This may be the point: The church likewise has a strong vision of the future called
the kingdom of God. What's more, that future vision should include the potential joy
that will rock the cosmos in celebration when more, and not fewer, people end up at-
tending God's big party. That vision of the future should influence us mightily in also
the present moment. If that bright vision of our future really did inform and animate
our present moment in the church, maybe lots of things would change, starting with

our willingness to take joy when more—and not fewer—people get saved. Maybe we should hope even this shrewd manager will be part of God's kingdom party. That is the side Jesus is on as he tells this parable and the previous three in Luke 15. We are either on Jesus's side or we stand with the sneering Pharisees whose narrow judgmentalism kicked off these parables to begin with.

Secondary Preaching Theme

All over the world politics has become ugly and very personal. We no longer disagree with representatives of another party; we hate them. We revile them. Yet here is Paul in 1 Timothy 2 encouraging Pastor Timothy to urge his people to pray for the well-being of kings and leaders. Even more, to give thanksgiving to God for them.

Of course, our hyper-partisan environment these days makes these words a tough pill to swallow for many. It is difficult to give thanks for someone you spend your days trashing and despising and loathing because of all he or she represents. But lest we think it was easier in Timothy's day to follow this than it is in our day, let's remember: Paul was referring to leaders in the Roman and Greek worlds, to Caesars who fancied themselves gods, to iron-fisted rulers intent on persecuting the church and wiping out the name of Jesus.

How can Paul do this? Because of everything else he writes in 1 Timothy 2:1-7. His eye is on the real God, the true leader, the real king, and the only true mediator between God and humanity, Jesus Christ. This Jesus gave himself for "all people," which echoes verse 1 when Paul calls upon Timothy to urge his people to pray and make intercession and offer up thanksgiving "for all people," including kings and authorities. Connect the dots in this short passage and you see Paul hold out the hope that Jesus can save even the ugly and idolatrous wannabe divine being known as the Caesar or two-bit, tin-plated lesser figures like kings named Herod or other lesser (but no less brutal) dignitaries in the empire.

Lots of things in life get relativized and put into their proper place and perspective when you see the big picture. When you see, as Paul did, Jesus high and lifted up and God the Father as ruling all things and all peoples . . . well, lots of lesser things in life recede to the background. Everything gets bathed in a different light, a holy light.

Benediction (from Psalm 79)

The Lord bless you and keep you.
We are, after all, your people, O God, and the sheep of your very own pasture. We will give you thanks forever, we will proclaim your praises from one generation to the next.
Go in peace. Amen.

September 29, 2019

Passages: Jeremiah 32:1-3a, 6-15; Psalm 91:1-6, 14-16; 1 Timothy 6:6-19;
Luke 16:19-31

Gathering Prayer

God of generosity, you call us to acknowledge the bounty of what we have and to share it.
Open our eyes to the abundance around us. Help us see our brothers and sisters in need.
Fill us with holy compassion, free us from our tendency to hoard, our fear of not having
enough, and our habit of self-justification. We ask you these things in the name of Jesus,
one without a place to lay his head. Amen.

Preaching Theme

This is difficult teaching! It all sounds beautiful: compassion, sharing, simplicity, and life together. In reality, though, speaking against our tendency to put our trust in riches can be a dangerous thing in our churches. I wonder if we could take the invitation that the lectionary gives us this week and allow it to give us courage. We could speak to our congregations from our own struggles with our cultural obsession, with having more no matter what the cost. We could speak to them about how we, like the rich man and his brothers, know what Jesus calls us to and yet we struggle. We allow fear, anxiety, and a desire to fit in to guide us and then we become angry if anyone dares to question it. Maybe this week we let the passage speak the prophetic word and we become the gentle shepherds who humbly and confessionally guide others into the depths of these words. Who knows, maybe someone in our pews might hear this difficult teaching and be transformed!

Secondary Preaching Theme

The middle of a siege is not where you expect to find a call to invest in the future of the land. In the midst of struggle we tend to conserve, to focus solely on surviving. It is human nature, a by-product of our evolutionary development. We are living in a season in church life where we feel besieged. Things continue to change all around us, our churches do not seem to be thriving, and we no longer have the power that we once held in society. The primary tendency would be to go into survival mode. What if we are being called to proclaim that God expects us to invest again? This week we might acknowledge that from the beginning of our story as the people of God we have been called to look toward the future with hope. There will be life again, growth again, transformation again, resurrection again; but we must be willing to invest, find the deeds of our place in the communities we serve and hold them tight, claim our ownership and our place, and begin proclaiming that we will indeed live!

Responsive Reading (Based on Psalm 91)

Because God is our refuge and our stronghold
We are not afraid of the terrors at night!

Because God will save us from the hunter's trap
    and from deadly sickness
We are not afraid of the terrors at night!

Because God will protect us with his pinions;
    find refuge under his wings, to protect us
We are not afraid of the terrors at night!

Because we've made the Lord our refuge,
    the Most High, our place of residence—
We are not afraid of the terrors at night!

Because the Lord will order his messengers to help us,
    to protect us wherever we go
We are not afraid of the terrors at night!

Because God's messengers will carry us
    with their own hands so we don't bruise our foot on a stone
We are not afraid of the terrors at night!

Because when we cry out God answers,
    during troubling times, old age, and sickness.
We are not afraid of the terrors at night!

Because God will show us salvation!
We are not afraid of the terrors at night!

Benediction

Now, may the God who calls us to share what we have without fear, the God who calls us to hope in the midst of despair, the God who calls us to a new day in the midst of the everyday, guide you, strengthen you, bless you, and keep you, today and in the days to come, Amen.

October 6, 2019

Passages: Lamentations 1:1-6; Lamentations 3:19-26 or Psalm 137;
2 Timothy 1:1-14; Luke 17:5-10

Gathering Prayer

God of hope, sometimes we ignore the reality that is around us. We would rather hide than face the pain, the loss, and the struggle. We would rather pretend that we have it all together, that we have no worries, and that all is well. By the power of the Holy Spirit, allow us to be a community of lament, confession, and vulnerability. Allow us to be such a place for one another and for the community around us. Fill us with hope and use us as a hope-full people, through Christ, our Lord. Amen.

Preaching Theme

Lament is not something we talk about often enough. These days, even at funerals, it is hard to lament. We would rather jump from celebration to celebration, as so many of us do at Holy Week, than face the reality of our lives and the lives of those around us. Lament is truth telling, is prophetic, and can be a healing agent. Communal lament reminds us that we are not alone but that the first step to healing is to acknowledge our need for it. This week we might encourage our congregations to think about their week and to name in their hearts or out loud the things that break their hearts, that make them weep. It is only then that we can truly hope, only then that the word of good news can find fertile ground.

Secondary Preaching Theme

Congregational leadership can be life-taking. This is something we as leaders tend not to want to talk about (see above), but I believe that we cannot miss the opportunity that the letter to Timothy provides us. The passage gives us a helpful blueprint to speak about the burden of leadership without sounding whiny or like we are asking for pity. The letter reminds us that the first seed of our calling to leadership is a call to follow Jesus. This call to follow Jesus is then made more specific by the laying on of hands, by the passing on of the Holy Spirit from one generation of leaders to another. This is a heavy set of hands, but again it is a reminder that our call to leadership is not ours. Finally it is grace that sustains our calling. Grace does not guarantee an easy life; instead it provides the needed presence of God through it all.

Responsive Reading (Psalm 137 and Lamentations)

God we find ourselves weary, weeping, and wondering.
God we hope for a new day!

God we find ourselves away from home, lost, and out of sorts.
God we hope for a new day!

God we find ourselves lonely in a crowd, hungry in a feast,
and thirsty in water overflowing.
God we hope for a new day!

God we find ourselves forgetting, erasing, and dismembering.
God we hope for a new day!

God we find ourselves voiceless, sightless, and heartless.
God we hope for a new day!

God we find ourselves . . .
God we hope for a new day!

Benediction

Now may the God of hope comfort you, give you voice, and guide you home. May the spirit of God provide memory, feasting, and vision. May Christ heal you, restore you, and bless you today and in the days to come, Amen.

October 13, 2019

Passages: Jeremiah 29:1, 4-7; Psalm 66:1-12; 2 Timothy 2:8-15;
Luke 17:11-19

Gathering Prayer

God of naming, calling, and sending, you encounter us along the way, sick, lost, and gifted. As we gather for worship today, remind us of who we are, say our name, and remind us of our reason for being. As we meet you in this place, join us together and help us see your healing, directing, and empowering work in our lives and in the lives of our brothers and sisters around us. Through Christ our Lord we pray, Amen.

Preaching Theme

There's an old saying that "familiarity breeds contempt." We gather for worship week to week singing the same songs, hearing the same announcements, and maybe even hearing a different version of the same sermon. No wonder after a while we might not even notice God's healing work among us. Luke's passage gives us much fodder for sermonizing, but I've always been curious about this so-called foreigner who returned. We are often hard toward the nine who did not come back, but maybe they did not realize that they were healed? Maybe they expected it since it is what Jesus was known to do? I think the foreigner returned because he was caught by surprise, because as he ran away with the others, he realized that he had no priest to go to.

Secondary Preaching Theme

I've lost count of the number of battles over words that I have gotten into. I love words and I believe that words matter. I also know that in a community words have the power to unite or to divide. The church seems to be a fertile place for battles over words. We often major in the minors, tear each other apart, and easily dismiss each other. The letter to Timothy reminds us that we need to be more attentive to our words. We need to make sure that as teachers and preachers we model the proper and life-giving use of words to build up, to heal, and to make peace in our communities and in our world.

In Jeremiah we have the opportunity to remind the community that we are gifted in ways to serve God and neighbor. As preachers, we need to use this time to help the community of faith see our gathering of worship and our life together as an opportunity to help us discover the ways that we are uniquely gifted and called. We might also discover some practical ways to grow in our gifts and to use them in ways that honor God.

Offering Invitation

People of God, today the lepers remind us to pay attention to the many ways that God is at work in our lives. As we give, may our generosity be rooted in the growing awareness of our healing and in our meeting Jesus in gratitude.

Benediction

Now may the healing power of Jesus surprise you, the awareness of your unique gifts guide you, the presence of the Holy Spirit empower you, and the blessing of God who is Father, Son, and Holy Spirit lead you to life abundant for you and those around you, Amen.

October 20, 2019

*Passages: Jeremiah 31:27-34; Psalm 119:97-104; 2 Timothy 3:14–4:5;
Luke 18:1-8*

Gathering Prayer

*Eternal God, you speak to us through prophets, apostles, and teachers. As we gather for
worship, may we hear your voice, pay attention to your instruction, and allow it to become
inscribed in our hearts. Take away all distractions and by the power of the Holy Spirit
allow us to become your word, your life, and your forgiveness for the life of the world.
Through Christ our Lord. Amen.*

Preaching Theme

Do we realize that God is still speaking? Today the scriptures give us the opportunity to help our congregation learn to hear God's voice in their everyday life. To
hear God's voice during the good times and during the bad times. To hear God's voice
in the places where they live, work, and play. Once they learn to hear God's voice,
we now must help our congregations learn to allow that voice to be recorded in our
souls. It is this recording that sustains us and helps us discern God's work in our lives.
It is also this recording of God's voice that facilitates our daily encounter with God in
scripture as the record of God's revelation in Jesus Christ.

The image that Jeremiah gives us of engraving as sign of identity provides a vivid
picture of what it looks like to be a people of God's word. If we do not encourage
people to expand their understanding of the word beyond Jesus and the word beyond
scripture, we miss an opportunity for our people to hear God and proclaim that it is
indeed pleasing!

Secondary Preaching Theme

Praying continuously is a challenge for all of us. We are busy, distracted, and
exhausted. "Life must be lived," we tell ourselves. Today Jesus gives us an interesting
and helpful picture of what it might mean to stay connected, not out of duty, but out
of perseverance, need, and desperation. God in turn will not be able to ignore the
plight. Like a child who cries continuously, our continuous prayer is impossible to

ignore. How can we help our congregations to persevere in their prayer life not only as community but also as individuals? Can we take time each day to "bother" God who is ready to hear?

Responsive Reading (Based on Psalm 119 and Jeremiah 31)

We love your instruction!
> We think about it constantly.
You are our God, and we are your people!

Your commandment makes us wiser than our enemies
> because it is always with us.
You are our God, and we are your people!

We have greater insight than all our teachers
> because we contemplate your laws.
You are our God, and we are your people!

We have more understanding than the elders
> because we guard your precepts.
You are our God, and we are your people!

We haven't set our feet on any evil path
> so we can make sure to keep your word.
You are our God, and we are your people!

We haven't deviated from any of your rules
> because you are the one who has taught us.
You are our God, and we are your people!

Your word is so pleasing to our taste buds—
> it's sweeter than honey in our mouth!
You are our God, and we are your people!

We are studying your precepts—
> that's why we hate every false path.
The Lord has forgotten all our wrongdoing
And will never again remember our sin.

Benediction

May the God who has engraved God's word within us, who has fed us with the feast of that word, and who has placed it as a guide for our path, bless us and keep us now and always, Amen!

"Praying In-Between"

Luke 18:1-8

O. Wesley Allen Jr.

Background Material: *The Gospel reading for this Sunday is the parable of the widow and the unjust judge. This parable is unique to Luke. Different exegetical methodologies will render different interpretations of the parable.*

A critical reading of verses 2-5 examines how the parable functioned independently as part of the early church's oral proclamation before it was embedded in the third Gospel. In such a setting, the parable can be read as a story directed to the church illustrating how it was to deal with unjust political powers. If the powers-that-be will not respond to the calls of the oppressed out of a sense of what is right, then the oppressed must be persistent in demanding justice. In this sense the parable calls the audience to endurance of purpose and offers hope that such endurance will result in justice. This emphasis can be seen in the judge's decision to grant the widow justice "so she may not wear me out." The Greek word translated as "wear out" can mean "strike one in the face." The image of an ancient widow striking a judge in the face to obtain a just decision in a court case is a compelling metaphor for the church's work in the arena of social justice.

Redaction and literary critical approaches that attend to the final form of the text and how it functions as a part of Luke's finished narrative will render a different sort of reading of the lection. The manner in which Luke contextualized the parable of the widow and the unjust judge changes its focus considerably. In 17:20 the Pharisees ask Jesus when the reign of God is coming. Jesus rejects the idea that the kingdom can be identified in terms of time or place. Instead, he says, "the kingdom of God is among you." This saying has often been read as a Lukan expression of realized eschatology. It is better read as though Luke is interpreting eschatology experientially instead of chronologically. God's future is an essential, eternal element of present Christian experience.

Luke presents Jesus as interpreting the parable of the widow and the unjust judge in terms of this experiential eschatology. It is not simply about dealing with different instances of injustice in the world. The parable is about praying for God's eschatological justice to reign on earth and how that future-oriented prayer should manifest itself in faithfulness.

In this Lukan context, the parable functions allegorically employing the logic of comparing the lesser (human) and the greater (divine). The judge is meant to represent God, not in terms of the judge's unjust character but in his final granting of justice to the widow. If an unjust judge will offer justice slowly, how much more quickly will our just God render justice? The comparison is theologically troubling in that it implies God must be coaxed to do good for those in need. But the instruction intended, as named in the opening (v. 1), is for the disciples to pray with persistence in an eschatological existence. Thus Luke uses "quickly" metaphorically, having more to do with the intensity of Christian existence than it does an actual temporal reference.

The following sermon attempts to name the theological complexity of the passage (without getting lost in it) while zooming in on the text's invitation to consider the relationship of prayer and eschatology. In today's mainline church, prayer is too often domesticated into a self-help discipline or a wish list for Santa God. And while eschatology plays a significant role in some conservative churches that take references to the parousia literally, most churches ignore it. To bring these two topics together in one sermon is to give hearers a chance to reflect on both anew.

Sermon: Ronnie Milsap, the country singer, was born blind. I have heard him tell of his grandmother leading him in near-constant prayer for healing. She took him from one tent meeting to the next, one faith healer to the next, trying to get him sight. Exorcisms were performed, hands were laid on his eyes. Praise and laments were lifted up to God in harmony. Day after day, week after week, year after year...and God did nothing.

Ronnie's grandmother questioned her faithfulness. She must've thought, "If I just had the faith of a mustard seed, God would give you sight. I must not be praying correctly. I must not be praying enough."

Our passage tells us that Jesus told the people around him a parable about their need to pray always and not to lose heart. He said, "In a certain city there was a judge who neither feared God nor had respect for people. In that city there was a widow who kept coming to him and saying, 'Grant me justice against my opponent.' For a while he refused; but later he said to himself, 'Though I have no fear of God and no respect for anyone, yet because this widow keeps bothering me, I will grant her justice, so that she may not wear me out by continually coming.'" And the Lord said, "Listen to what the unjust judge says. And will not God grant justice to his chosen ones who cry to him day and night? Will he delay long in helping them? I tell you, he will quickly grant justice to them. And yet, when the Son of Man comes, will he find faith on earth?"

This parable is built on the ancient logic of lesser to greater. We're familiar with this logic from other places in scripture. If earthly parents give good things to their parents, how much better will be that which our heavenly parent gives us? If earthly rulers have power, how much more power does the almighty wield? The logic is simple: if lesser humans do something good, how much better the greater God will do? So the logic in this parable goes: if an unjust judge will slowly give in to the widow's persistent pleas for justice, how much more quickly will God give in to our persistent pleas for justice?

But that logic leaves an awfully bad taste in our mouths and raises all sorts of questions. What kind of a God would require us to be annoying before granting us justice? "Jesus loves me this I know, as long as I bug him so?"

Ronnie Milsap's grandmother questioned her faithfulness. Like many of us, perhaps she also thought something like, "If I just had the faith of a mustard seed, God would give you sight. I must not be praying correctly. I must not be praying enough." But Ronnie questioned God. How much prayer, how much faith does God need before God will grant sight to an innocent little boy?

Whenever we bow our heads in prayer, we are making a theological statement about the nature of God by what we decide to pray. We have prayer disciplines, prayer chains, prayer warriors, prayer vigils. We are trying to maximize the power of prayer. All of this implies that God, at best, must be persuaded to be just and, at worst, must be manipulated. And it says that prayer is the method of manipulation. Maybe God will respond if I pray longer—the tortoise beats the hare every time, you know. Maybe God will respond if we pray together—there's power in numbers. Maybe God will listen if I am on my knees offering up silent petitions…or if I am standing with my hands outstretched and my mouth speaking in tongues.

Our approach to prayer at one moment turns God into a Santa Claus and the next transforms the Deity into a puzzle box filled with blessing. If we're just good enough to stay off God's naughty list, we'll get what we need. How we pray and how much we pray will show how good we are. Or if we are just persistent enough, we will unlock God's heart and find hidden there a treasure of mercy and love and justice.

This is the God this parable seems to present. A God who leaves a bad taste in my mouth and leaves blindness in Ronnie Milsap's eyes. If I had been Luke's editor, I would have suggested he either rewrite the parable or omit it from his Gospel altogether. But there it is stuck right at the beginning of the eighteenth chapter. Too many people have seen it there to try and get rid of it now. So we have to deal with it. It is part of "our book."

Perhaps if we look at the parable more closely, we may see it differently and find a different view of prayer and of God offered to us. Jesus doesn't offer the parable and leave it hanging there for us to make whatever we want of it. He knows that to speak of prayer is to speak of God. Too often preachers don't trust stories to do their job and explain them away like someone trying to explain why a joke is funny. But some stories must be contextualized or they can mean things they shouldn't. So Jesus gives us a context to hear the story in. After narrating the judge's slow and reluctant response to the widow, he says, "Listen to what the unjust judge says. And will not God grant justice to his chosen ones who cry to him day and night? Will he delay long in helping them? I tell you, he will quickly grant justice to them. And yet, *when the Son of Man comes*, will he find faith on earth?" (emphasis added).

When the Son of Man comes? Where did that come from? What's that all about? It seems like Jesus forgot what he was talking about and went off on a tangent. I know you aren't familiar with any preachers who ever do that. But maybe Jesus doesn't commit a non sequitur here. Maybe this odd reference to the Son of Man coming is the key to the whole parable. Jesus doesn't want us to hear the parable as talking about any old justice but the justice that comes when Jesus returns in final victory. Jesus wants the disciples to hear the parable in an eschatological context.

Now I just broke one of the rules I give to my students in preaching class. I tell them not to use three-dollar seminary words in sermons. They're show-off words. And "eschatological" is certainly one of those words. But there's just no better word for what Jesus is talking about than eschatology. Eschatology comes from the Greek word *eschaton*, which means end. So eschatology is the study of the end, specifically the end of time, the end of history, Jesus's return, the resurrection of the dead, the rapture, not the Alpha but the Omega.

Eschatology is important to talk about because it appears on practically every page of the New Testament. We most identify it with the book of Revelation and its wild apocalyptic imagery, but eschatology is painted all over the Gospels and Paul as well. A foundational belief of the early Christians was that God is in control of the future and its ultimate end and that the teaching, ministry, death, and resurrection of Jesus Christ foreshadow what that end is going to be like.

But we Christians are a dumb lot. We take poetic lyrics and prophetic visions and turn them into bulleted to-do lists for God. Every generation of Christians has had its version of *The Late Great Planet Earth* or the Left Behind series, and every one of them has been wrong. Every time a new century has begun, there have been people gathered on some hillside or on top of some building on December 31 at 11:59 p.m. waiting expectantly for Jesus to appear with the stroke of midnight (although I'm not sure which time zone Jesus would choose). We want to take God's promise to be out before us, God's call for us to lean into the future faithfully, and make it concrete and specific and secure…and known. We have mistaken biblical prophecy for a crystal ball of predictions, and the mystery of God is diminished.

The coming of the Son of Man is not an event you can synchronize your watch to or note in your date book or set an alarm for on your smartphone. It's not about chronology; it's about divine eternity touching human temporality. "When the Son of Man comes" is a Christian experience. We Christians live in the already-not yet. Christ has already been born and lived and died and rose for us. Christ has already given to us salvation. We already experience Christ's constant, loving presence in the Holy Spirit. *But* the world still experiences birth pangs of the Christ event. We have yet to see peace cover the earth. We have yet to see an end to sickness and death. We have yet to live in the fullness of the reign of God. We have yet to live in the reality of a just world for all of God's creatures. "Jesus came" and "Jesus is coming" is a great paradox of our faith. Already-not yet.

It is like driving on a country road in the middle of a dark night. Over the next hill we can see a car's headlights beaming. We are already experiencing the car. We are switching to our low beams. Moving a little more to the right. But we have yet to meet the car completely. This is Christian existence. Christ's light shines in our lives already and we are shaped by it. But there is yet more of Christ to know and love and experience. Already-not yet.

Today's parable is spoken in the already of the Christian relationship with God expressed in prayer but addresses the not yet of God's justice being fully manifested on earth.

And the Lord said, "Listen to what the unjust judge says. And will not God grant justice to his chosen ones who cry to him day and night? Will he delay long in helping them? I tell you, he will quickly grant justice to them. And yet, when the Son of Man comes, will he find faith on earth?"

While for Ronnie Milsap the parable of the widow and the unjust judge would rightfully raise questions about God's judgment, Jesus uses the parable to raise questions about our faithfulness. But not in the way that Ronnie's grandmother asked the question. She hoped that if she prayed in just the right way, God would turn into a fairy godparent and grant her wish for Ronnie. It is an understandable desire. When a loved one suffers, who wouldn't want God to fix it? But Luke's view of God and prayer rejects the fixer-upper God. Luke raises a different question about our faithfulness. Luke wants us asking ourselves, in the experience of God not only being with us but being out before us, have we been faithful in our praying forward to justice? Not justice praying *for* justice but praying *forward to* justice.

In our prayers we mention those who are discriminated against, but have we prayed them into God's future? Our prayer chains lift up those who are ill and lonely, but have we carried those people toward God's not yet? Our pastoral prayers speak of the war and Iraq and unrest in Palestine and Israel, but have we called those situations forward into God's peace? In our litanies we utter our desire for guidance for our religious and political leaders, but have we prayed our leaders toward God's desire? We cry out in lament concerning pollution and global warming and drought and famine and extinction, but have our tears flowed forth into a new stewardship for God's creation? "And yet, when the Son of Man comes, will he find faith on earth?" Will God find us praying forward to justice?

I believe praying in private, saying grace at the dinner table, gathering each Sunday to pray, are all important expressions of the Christian faith. But we are also called to pray forward to God's not yet. Those in the civil rights movement knew this. They didn't just gather for worship where they sang and prayed and listened to sermons. And they didn't just go out and protest at the segregated lunch counters and schools and bus lines. Their protests *were* prayer meetings. They marched to Selma singing spirituals to God so that the world could overhear their prayer and be moved toward a God who shows no partiality. They gathered at the mall in Washington, DC, and prayed their dream to God in a way that the world could envision God's reign. They linked arms and lifted up God's names as police dogs and fire hoses were turned on them in the streets of Birmingham so that the world would feel God's rage. To move the world toward justice is to pray forward to the coming of the Son of Man.

Leigh Raiford has studied photographs from the civil rights movement and analyzed the way they conveyed the deepest convictions of those invested in the struggle.[1] One photograph he looks at has the caption "Come Let Us Build a New World Together." It was taken at a segregated swimming pool. Two men knelt on either side of a young girl as they prayed at the edge of the pool before they were forcibly removed. In the photograph you can't see the girl's face—her head is bowed so low with sorrow and piety that only the top of the head is visible. But what you can see clearly are her hands. They are wrapped around her knee with one finger pointing forward. Raiford claims the finger serves as a compass. I know what it's pointing to— her constant north. You know what it's pointing to. She's praying. She is praying for justice. She is praying justice forward. Her finger is pointing to God's not yet... but soon and very soon.

October 27, 2019

Passages: Joel 2:23-32; Psalm 65; 2 Timothy 4:6-8, 16-18; Luke 18:9-14

Call to Worship (Based on Psalm 65)

Shout for joy and break out in song!
Sing praise to the God of all living things!
We marvel at the one who establishes the mountains!
Sing praise to the God of all living things!
We are in awe at the one who calms the seas!
Sing praise to the God of all living things!
Come, let us worship the giver of life!
Sing praise to the God of all living things! Amen!

Preaching Theme

This Sunday, many congregations across the United Methodist Church will gather and celebrate All Saints' Day, observed yearly on November 1. As United Methodists, we celebrate All Saints' Day as "an opportunity to give thanks for all those who have gone before us in faith."[2] Often, we lift up the names of those who have died, especially in the last year, and remember them through the lighting of a candle or the ringing of a bell as names are shared. While grief and sorrow are present in the ritual of remembering, we also give thanks for their lives and the ways we have been impacted by the lives of those who have gone before us. Trusting that God who has been faithful before will be faithful to us now, we can celebrate All Saints' Day with hope.

The author of 2 Timothy reminds us of this, inviting the readers to reflect with him on his own life—the hardships and the struggles, the abandonment he now experiences writing presumably from a prison cell, and the hope the author finds in Christ. As the author writes about his nearing death, we have the opportunity to pause and to reflect on our own lives, asking ourselves if we, too, have lived a life worth living—fighting the good fight, finishing the race, keeping the faith (2 Tim 4:7).

There will be those in one's community who are close to death—those experiencing old age and the challenges to the mind and body that come with this process, as well as those battling cancer and other diseases. And there will be others who are

118 –

experiencing strength in mind and body, who live without anxiety of what tomorrow might bring. At every stage of life, this text can challenge and encourage us to examine our lives and draw on the inspiration of others. Are there people in our communities, both present and of the past, who have lived as the author commends us to live? In what ways? What can we learn from their examples? Even as we celebrate All Saints' Day, might we turn our focus from death to the life we are called to live—that we, too, would receive the wreath for righteousness at the end of our days!

Secondary Preaching Theme

The lectionary text from the Gospel according to Luke also challenges us to examine our lives, whether we are living with righteousness. In this passage, Jesus introduces two people who are praying: the Pharisee and the tax collector. Though both are engaging in the act of prayer, Jesus describes them as having very different practices. The Pharisee celebrates himself, using prayer as a way of distancing himself from those he deems lower than himself. The tax collector humbles himself. Though the Pharisee might have lived his life according to the rules of law, the attitude with which the tax collector prays is what separates the two characters, leading Jesus to name the tax collector, and not the Pharisee, as justified.

Especially in light of All Saints' Day, this text can challenge and inspire us to consider not only our actions but also our attitudes. Are we living lives trying to get ahead of others, sometimes even stepping on people who society casts as lower than us, for our own glory? Are we being like the Pharisee in our faith and in the ways our faith is lived out? Or can we strive to be more like the tax collector, who recognizes his own humanity and pleads to God for mercy?

Benediction (Based on Joel 2:23-32)

O children of God, rejoice and be glad in the Lord your God, for God has been and will be faithful to you. Go forth in abundance, for the Lord your God will be by your side. Go forth living lives of righteousness, for the spirit of the living God will be upon you in all your ways. O children of God, rejoice and be glad! Go forth!

November 3, 2019

Passages: Habakkuk 1:1-4; 2:1-4; Psalm 119:137-44; 2 Thessalonians 1:1-4, 11-12; Luke 19:1-10

Gathering Prayer (Based on Psalm 119:137-44)

O God, you remind us of your faithfulness time and time again. Though we are weak, you gather us in this space, setting our feet on your foundation of righteousness and truth. In your laws, you remain trustworthy; in your word, you remain steadfast; in your instruction, you remain true. Be with us now and inspire us, as you have inspired generations before us, breathing into us new life! In Christ Jesus, we pray, Amen.

Preaching Theme

Do you ever find yourself feeling like you have to justify your worth? It seems as if everywhere we turn, there is something or someone willing and ready to tear us down. We often get messages that remind us of our failures and inadequacies, from the media or our peers or society as a whole. We're not pretty enough or smart enough or fast enough or tall enough. By the world's standards, we are rarely ever enough.

Jesus, however, challenges this notion of not being enough. In the passage from the Gospel according to Luke, we find Jesus entering Jericho and we are introduced to Zacchaeus, who was "a wee little man, a wee little man was he!" Aside from his stature, the text tells us many other things about Zacchaeus. For example, Zacchaeus held power, being described as "a ruler among tax collectors" (v. 2). Zacchaeus had status, being described as "rich" (v. 2). It appears he had heard something about this man named Jesus, or else he would not have put in the effort to climb the tree simply to "see who Jesus was" (v. 3), and it also appears that he fit the stereotype of what we have come to know tax collectors to be: a cheater and a sinner.

As he comes down the tree upon Jesus's beckon, Zacchaeus is reminded of what the world thinks of him. The passage tells us that those who saw him walk with Jesus "grumbled" (v. 7) and called him "sinner" (v. 7). Zacchaeus, in his effort to justify himself, stops and appears to plead his case before the Lord—"But see Jesus? I do this and this and this!"

While Zacchaeus focuses on his actions, specifically what he does to deem himself worthy to be in Christ's presence, Jesus seems to ignore Zacchaeus's résumé, not even addressing what Zacchaeus says. Instead Jesus reminds him, and all those in the crowd, that salvation is not earned but freely given. It is in Zacchaeus's identity as an Israelite, as a child of the covenant, as a son of Abraham, that makes him worthy.

How might our lives be different if we did not hold ourselves or those around us to the standards of this world, but rather saw each person with sacred worth as a beloved child of God? Would we sneer at Zacchaeus like those in the crowd calling him a sinner? Would we feel the need to justify ourselves with padded résumés? Or could we be freed to live into the fullness of our identities as children of God, not stepping on each other or making ourselves appear worthy?

Secondary Preaching Theme

If the passage from the Gospel according to Luke reminds us of our identity as children of God, then the passage from 2 Thessalonians might portray for us the response from the freedom that comes in that affirmed identity. For the author of this letter, it is "only right [to give thanks to God] because your faithfulness is growing by leaps and bounds, and the love that all of you have for each other is increasing" (v. 3). But the author also makes it clear that these reasons to give thanks are not because of the work done by the people of Thessalonica. Rather, it is by God's power.

And so, we, too, might hear the author's prayer, that God would make us worthy of the call. As we have been called beloved children of God, grafted into the family of believers, much like the converts of Thessalonica, might we also be encouraged and challenged to allow reason for those around us to give thanks to God.

Benediction (Based on 2 Thessalonians 1:11-12)

Go forth from this place assured of your identity in the living Christ—that your life would give all glory and honor to the one who is creator, sustainer, and redeemer. And go forth trusting that the grace of our Lord, Jesus Christ, and the great love of God, and the sweet communion of the Holy Spirit will be by your side every step along your journey. Amen.

November 10, 2019

Passages: Haggai 1:15b–2:9; Psalm 98; 2 Thessalonians 2:1-5, 13-17; Luke 20:27-38

Call to Worship (Based on Psalm 98)

Sing to the Lord a new song, shout triumphantly to the Lord, all the earth!
We will be happy! We will rejoice! We will sing our praises!
Come, sing to the Lord a new song!
We will sing our praises with the lyre!
Come, sing to the Lord a new song!
We will sing our praises with trumpets and horns!
Come, sing to the Lord a new song!
With all creation, we will sing!
Sing to the Lord a new song!
We will shout triumphantly to the Lord!

Preaching Theme

As we get closer to Christ's impending death and resurrection in the Gospel according to Luke, we find that there are more and more questions about the resurrection and the end of the world. It is almost as if the author of this Gospel is preparing the readers for all that is still to come in the narrative. It is in this vein that we approach Luke 20, as the Sadducees approach Jesus with a question about the resurrection. They ask a hypothetical question, an absurd one at that, and wait for Jesus's response. And while they put the focus of their question about the resurrection on the woman and her seven husbands, Jesus responds by putting the focus of the resurrection on God. In this way, Jesus reorients their understanding about the resurrection.

I remember a time when I was playing on my middle school basketball team—"playing" is actually too generous of a description. I remember a time when I was the backup to the backup on my middle school basketball team. In other words, while I was officially a member of the team, I hardly ever played. On one specific occasion, however, I remember we were losing by so many points in the fourth quarter that Coach finally put me in, and did I make most use of my time in the game! I scored something like fifteen points and was getting rebounds; I was dribbling between my legs and passing the ball around my back! On the car ride home, I could not stop talking about my performance to my dad, until I realized he wasn't as excited for me as I thought he should have been. When I asked him why he wasn't as excited as I was, he responded wondering if I was missing the point of the game...at the end of the day, my team had lost.

I wonder what it is about our human nature that limits our worldview to be centered around ourselves. We tend to make our jobs or our careers about ourselves as opposed to the greater good; we make our studies about our advancement rather than the learning or the knowledge; we make service about ourselves and the number of community service hours that could be accrued; we even make church about ourselves and our visibility or our dreams. We act like the Sadducees who made the resurrection about us, humans, when in reality, the resurrection is about the living God and God's power and victory over death. What might it look like to reorient our thoughts and our actions, even our very being, to be focused on God as opposed to ourselves?

Secondary Preaching Theme

Both the passage from Haggai and the passage from 2 Thessalonians fit nicely with this theme of the focus being on God and not on humans. In Haggai, the prophet relays the Lord's words to Joshua, the high priest, reminding Joshua that it will be the Lord who will bring renewal and restoration to Jerusalem. And so, Joshua does not need to be afraid; rather, the Lord tells him to "be strong" (v. 4). Likewise, the 2 Thessalonians passage challenges the readers to not be confused by words of other people about the end of days. Instead, the author reminds the readers that it is God who first chose us, and that "God called [us] through our good news so [we] could possess the honor of our Lord Jesus Christ" (v. 14). In both cases, our focus needs to be on God and God's redeeming work, not the work of human hands.

Benediction (Based on Psalm 98)

Go forth from this place, singing unto the Lord a new song! Go forth, trusting that God remembers God's love for you, that God will remain faithful to you. Go forth, relying on the promise of God's justice to be established in the world. Go forth!

November 17, 2019

Passages: Isaiah 65:17-25; Isaiah 12; 2 Thessalonians 3:6-13; Luke 21:5-19

Gathering Prayer (Based on Isaiah 12)

O God, indeed be our salvation. As you draw us into this space, may we put our trust in you, for we will not fear. Be present and among us, God, reminding us of your faithfulness and your wondrous deeds. We praise you, we exalt you, we worship you, now and forever, Amen.

Preaching Theme

In the passage from the Gospel according to Luke, Jesus paints for the people a terrifying picture of the end times. The world will be overrun by war and chaos, and followers of Jesus will be persecuted for their faith. There will be betrayals and death, wars and rebellions, great earthquakes and wide-scale food shortages and epidemics! It might be easy to wonder if we might be living in these times; I confess that there are days that I do. One needs only to open a newspaper, turn on the TV or radio, or see an update on social media to be overwhelmed by the many headlines of death and destruction. Wars are happening around us and the threat of war is always imminent. Natural disasters seem common and the number of those in need of food or housing or health care continue to climb. How could we live in our world and not wonder if the end time is near?

And then we are reminded of Jesus's response to the crowd when they ask him for a sign to know when all these will take place. He says, "Watch out that you aren't deceived" (v. 8) and then, "Don't be alarmed" (v. 9). I wonder if in these two words of instruction, Jesus is in fact nudging us to not worry so much about the end days, for the end will come as nature runs its natural course. Instead, Jesus is challenging us to focus on these lives that we are called to live while on earth.

Jesus makes it clear that the road will not be easy, but he promises that he will be with us. Rather than relying on our own will or strength (v. 14), Jesus will provide the "words and wisdom" (v. 15) to go against our adversaries. The end of the world will come…someday. In the meantime, let us stay firm in our faiths as we live our lives until that day.

Secondary Preaching Theme

There appears to be a sharp contrast between the themes of the texts for this week, specifically between the words of Isaiah 65:17-25 and Luke 21:5-19. While Jesus describes a world full of death and destruction in the Gospel according to Luke, the psalmist paints a picture of the new heaven and the new earth to come. In this image, there is joy and gladness, quite contrary to the image depicted by Jesus in the Luke passage.

And while the text from 2 Thessalonians appears to be out of place with these other passages, I wonder if the author of 2 Thessalonians is meaning to ground us as we live out our lives. Rather than addressing what could be or what is to come, the author of 2 Thessalonians reminds the readers, both those who received the letter and those of us who read it now, of their commitment to a disciplined life. I wonder if this text is reminding us that until the end of the world comes, life does indeed go on, and it is our responsibility to continue doing what we are called to do. In this case, the author uses the example to work, but what might it be for us? To work? To love? To share?

Pastoral Prayer (Based on Isaiah 12 and Isaiah 65:17-25)

O God, you draw us near, for you are good and your love endures forever. You cover us in your love and your grace, and your glorious deeds are proclaimed throughout the world. And yet, there are times when we are afraid, when we hurt, when we cry, and when we are lost. Be our strength and our shield, that we might turn to you, putting our trust in you.

O God, you have promised a new heaven and a new earth, a place of joy and gladness. As we look toward that day with expectancy, listen to the sounds of your people crying and hear our prayers. For those who grieve the loss of life, both young and old, we pray. For those without houses and homes, and for those without enough to eat, we pray. For those searching for work, and those in the midst of violence, we pray. Lord, in your mercy, hear our prayers.

Grant us the assurance, O God, that we will indeed be glad and rejoice forever. It is in the holy and powerful name of Jesus Christ, we pray, Amen.

November 24, 2019–Christ the King Sunday

Passages: Jeremiah 23:1-6; Luke 1:68-79; Colossians 1:11-20; Luke 23:33-43

Responsive Prayer of Gathering (Based on Luke 1:68-79)

Bless the Lord God of Israel because God has come to help and has delivered God's people.

God has raised up a mighty Savior for us in David's house, as promised through the mouths of holy prophets long ago.

God has brought salvation from our enemies and from the power of all those who hate us.

God has shown the mercy promised to our ancestors, and remembered the holy covenant, the solemn pledge made to our ancestor Abraham.

God has granted that we would be rescued from the power of our enemies

So that we could serve God without fear, in holiness and righteousness in God's eyes, for as long as we live.

Because of our God's deep compassion, the dawn from heaven will break upon us,

God will give light to those who are sitting in darkness and in the shadow of death, to guide us on the path of peace.

Come let us worship the Lord!

Preaching Theme

Jesus's ability to forgive is astounding. He forgives those who crucify and mock him in the midst of his suffering. He extends mercy to the thief hanging alongside him. Jesus's practice of forgiveness here builds on a ministry of forgiveness throughout Luke's Gospel. As an embodiment of the kingdom of God, Jesus shows us that forgiveness is a sign of God's reign. In the New Testament, the language used for "forgiveness" has a root that carries connotations of being released or loosed.[1] Forgiveness releases both the one who has been wronged and the one who acted wrongly from a cycle of pain and bondage that can eat away at life, robbing people of joy and peace.

In Luke's version of the crucifixion narrative we are introduced to two thieves who hang on crosses next to Jesus. Tradition has named the "good" thief who asks for Jesus to remember him, Dismas. Now an organization called Dismas Fellowship provides an alternative worship service for ex-offenders whose conditions of release do not allow them to attend regular worship. One of the foundations of worship in Dismas Fellowship is that all stand in need of forgiveness from God and from others. The power of Jesus to forgive is life changing for those who are living with the consequences of harming others in the aftermath of incarceration. The Circles of Support and Accountability program creates a community around ex-offenders to stop the cycle of recidivism and help restore those who have served their sentence into broader society.

Our present political climate and social media bullies nurture a culture focused on retaliation and getting even. Viewing forgiveness as a sign of God's kingdom encourages us to live into this eschatological promise as a form of witness. The power of Christ makes forgiveness possible!

Secondary Preaching Theme

Jeremiah speaks of Babylonian exile and the eventual restoration for a remnant of Judah. The sins of Judah's kings and leaders are Judah's downfall. These shepherds have failed to care for God's sheep, and God is moved to act. God will gather the remaining scattered sheep and raise up a wise and righteous shepherd so that the sheep no longer need to be afraid. The perils of poor leadership are all too familiar. When a company goes bankrupt or an organization fails, the president or CEO is often fired, but others also suffer in the form of lost jobs or from the company's inability to make good on corporate promises. A recent news account tells of a prominent bridal retailer going out of business and leaving brides in tears because they paid for dresses that will never be delivered.[2]

In our text Jeremiah warns that the consequences for Judah will be horrific. However, God is not content to stand aside and watch unfaithful kings lead Judah away from faithful living and right relationships. This is good news! When earthly leaders fail, God will provide care and direction for God's people and at the right time will raise up a new leader whose reign will be marked by wisdom and justice.

Prayer of Confession

Merciful Christ,
Your reign is marked by self-giving love and new life. You extended forgiveness even while suffering on the cross. We call ourselves "Christian," but too often we harbor resentment and seek revenge against those who have wronged us. Grant us wisdom to recognize the limits of our judgment. May your Spirit empower us to forgive others in your name. Rule in our hearts and lives until your kingdom comes on earth.

Benediction

Christ the king has rescued you from the reign of darkness and brought you into his kingdom! May your lives reflect the light of Christ in your work, school, homes, and neighborhoods. As we move from worship into the world, let us serve Christ with joy and thanksgiving.

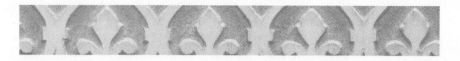

December 1, 2019–First Sunday of Advent

Passages: Isaiah 2:1-5; Psalm 122; Romans 13:11-14; Matthew 24:36-44

Gathering Prayer

God of all time,
In this season of darkness, of short days and long nights, we thank you for drawing your
people into your light this day. We join our voices with the faithful in all times and places.
We expectantly await your advent in our midst.

Preaching Theme

Some years ago, the Left Behind book series that described life on earth following the rapture of faithful believers was popular among Christians. While the books made for exciting reading, the events they portray are only conjecture. Matthew's Gospel text for today reminds us that no one knows when the day or hour will come for Christ's return, not the hosts of heaven or Jesus himself. Only God knows when and exactly how the return of Jesus will unfold. Nevertheless, Jesus calls his followers to stay alert, reminding them of the events that unfolded in the time of Noah, where people did not heed God's warning and kept going with business as usual. The first fat drops of rain began hitting their noses. Huddled in their tents, they likely didn't begin to panic until the waters started to rise. Jesus doesn't want his followers to be taken unaware. Jesus calls us to stay alert and to live like Jesus could come back at any time. As the country music song puts it, we should "live like we're dying."[1] And the Apostle Paul says in Romans 13:11, "The hour has already come for you to wake up from your sleep."

The 2015 Oscar-winning movie *Spotlight* centers around the actions of a group of reporters dedicated to telling the story of children abused by Boston-area priests that unfolded over decades. In the film, the church is portrayed at best as turning a blind eye to the abuse and at worst as enabling abusive and troubled priests to continue to hurt children. While this film focused on the Catholic Church, all denominations have struggled with a legacy of complacency when it comes to harmful actions such as abuse, cultural genocide, racism, and sexism. When the light of Christ shines on these actions, we come face to face with the truth of who we are and our deep need for Jesus Christ to save us.

Two thousand years of waiting may have lulled the church into slumber, but the season of Advent provides an opportunity to hear Christ's call like an alarm clock calling us to get up and start with the day. How might the church employ the light of Christ in our neighborhoods and community? How is Jesus getting our attention, and in what areas do our lives and families need to move from darkness and into light?

Secondary Preaching Theme

The passages from Isaiah and Psalm 122 envision a world of peace where God rules the world with a word from Jerusalem. How challenging it is to hear these verses given the state of Jerusalem today, marked with militarized zones and interreligious fighting. Jesus calls us to be people of peace, people who turn weapons of war into tools for nourishing and sustaining people. We join the psalmist in praying for peace in Jerusalem, but violence is not only a distant problem. Our schools, neighborhoods, towns, and cities are rocked with violence of all kinds from cyber-bullying to mass shootings. In the face of gun violence, some police departments have engaged in gun buy-back programs where people are paid to take often-unregistered firearms off the street. Some years ago the guns from such a program in Washington, DC, were melted down and turned into a sculpture, *Guns into Plowshares,* which now stands in front of a police station, reminding police officers and those who visit the station of alternatives to violence.

Prayer of Confession

Holy God,
You call us to be a people of peace, to walk in your light and live by the example of Jesus as we eagerly await his return. But over time our good intentions fade. We lose hope and return to old patterns that lead to the way of death and darkness. Rather than following Jesus's example, we often act in ways that hurt others and ourselves. In this season of Advent, we often choose indulgent pleasures of the moment rather than forbearance and sharing with those in need. Wake us up, God! Remind us of your promises! Wrap us in your light and love so that we might have the courage to follow the way of Jesus until he comes again.

Benediction

The night is almost over and the day is near! May the Spirit turn you away from the darkness and toward the light and love of God. May you live as people of the day as agents of Christ's love and peace in the world.

December 8, 2019–Second Sunday of Advent

Passages: Isaiah 11:1-10; Psalm 72:1-7, 18-19; Romans 15:4-13; Matthew 3:1-12

Gathering Prayer

As people gathered to hear John the Baptist in the wilderness, we come to worship longing for changed hearts and lives. Holy Spirit come among us! Cleanse us and nurture us that our lives might bear fruit for the kingdom of God.

Preaching Theme

Organization and decluttering expert Marie Kondo believes that organizing your home and belongings can change your life. The process starts with ruthlessly examining one's possessions and asking whether each item in one's home from socks to books and artwork "sparks joy."[2] If the item doesn't spark joy, it should go. In today's text, John the Baptist calls us to clean up our lives.

In Matthew 3:1-12, we meet John, a prophet with tastes in clothes and food after the style of the great Old Testament prophets. His message is clear, "Change your hearts and lives! Here comes the kingdom of heaven!" While Jesus's central message will be essentially the same as John's, the Gospel writer is careful to portray John as a forerunner of Jesus, one who prepares the way for and is subordinate to Jesus and not the messiah himself.[3] As Wes Allen puts it, "John *announces* the coming judgment. Jesus, on the other hand, *is* the eschatological judgment. John baptizes with water (like cleansing in the form of washing the surface of something), but Jesus baptizes with fire (like the purification in the form of refining or smelting metal to remove unwanted elements)."[4]

Jesus comes into the world to save us, but he sees us as we truly are—works in progress, diamonds in the rough. Part of salvation means letting Jesus evaluate our lives, all that we are and all that we do, and inviting him to change the parts of our lives that do not spark joy, the areas of life that are broken and hurting. Allowing Jesus to change us is the first step along a lifelong path of sanctification. Jesus sifts through our lives and behaviors, decluttering and burning away everything that is harmful and broken, everything that gets in the way of a life of joy. This process is difficult; it is the process of an alcoholic giving up her old drinking buddies to attend an AA meeting, of a workaholic setting strict boundaries around checking e-mail at home, or of marriage partners seeking counseling after betrayal.

If decluttering and organizing household belongings can change one's outlook, how much more can the power of Jesus Christ bring true transformation to lives, homes, and relationships!

Secondary Preaching Theme

The longings attested to in Isaiah 11 and Psalm 72 could be echoed by people today. Like Israel, we long for wise and righteous leaders, justice for poor and needy ones, and safety for all children. While we have a foretaste of resurrection and new life in Jesus, we are still waiting for the complete fulfillment of God's promises. It can be helpful in this season of Advent with shorter days and longer nights to look for signs of God's in-breaking kingdom in our world even as we continue to wait for Christ's return. Signs of hope are everywhere. Started in 2014 under the leadership of Dr. Jonathan Palant, "the Dallas Street Choir offers a musical outlet for those experiencing homelessness and severe disadvantage."[5] This group encourages people living in shelters or on the street, those who are often marginalized, to share their voices and musical gifts in ways that show us a glimpse of the kingdom of God, a place where all will have access to beauty and where every voice matters.

Prayer of Confession

Saving Christ,
We confess that our lives often do not bear the fruit that you desire. We ignore those in need. We choose violence instead of the way of peace. We squander your good gifts and waste the earth's resources. We judge our neighbors rather than extend mercy. Change our hearts and lives! Burn away all the behaviors and patterns that stifle joy and flourishing. Give us hearts and lives that are centered on your word.

Words of Assurance

The prophet reminds us,
A shoot will grow up from the stump of Jesse;
a branch will sprout from his roots.
The Lord's spirit will rest upon him,
a spirit of wisdom and understanding,
a spirit of planning and strength,
a spirit of knowledge and fear of the Lord.

The peoples and creatures of the earth will not harm or destroy anywhere on God's holy mountain and the earth will be filled with the knowledge of the Lord, just as the water covers the sea.

Benediction

May the transforming power of the Holy Spirit come into your hearts and lives, clearing away the clutter so that joy can flourish and bear the fruits of hope and peace in our world.

December 15, 2019–Third Sunday of Advent

Passages: Isaiah 35:1-10; Psalm 146:5-10 or Luke 1:46b-55; James 5:7-10; Matthew 11:2-11

Gathering Prayer

Jesus is coming! We gather to prepare the way with prayer and song. Our lives are thirsty and dry; may the Spirit fill our worship with hopeful expectation of the saving presence of God. Renew us, God; refresh us with streams of mercy and grace.

Preaching Theme

John the Baptist's question in Matthew 11:3 may strike us as strange. How can John doubt Jesus's identity after prophesying his arrival? This is not a matter of doubt, but a way for Matthew to affirm and strengthen Jesus's messianic identity.[6] When John asks if Jesus is "the one who is to come," Jesus tells John's followers to report what they have seen and heard about the things Jesus has done. Jesus is fulfilling messianic prophecies. Those with illnesses and disabilities are being healed, the dead are raised, and the poor have good news. Even John's supposed doubt becomes an opportunity to witness to the miraculous and wonderful things Jesus is doing.

Doubt can be a normal part of a life of faith. When Mother Teresa's posthumous private writings were released, many were stunned to read about her decades-long dark night of the soul, in which she longed for but did not experience God's presence in her life.[7] Despite her doubt, Mother Teresa did not waiver in her practices of faith and ministry to desperately poor people. Even in the midst of doubt our lives can bear witness to belief.

The first part of the Gospel passage focuses on John's question of Jesus's identity, but in the second part Jesus helps to situate John and his powerful ministry heralding the way of Jesus in relation to the transformative power of the kingdom of God to lift up the least. The verses immediately following our lection offer a word of warning to those who reject John and Jesus.

Secondary Preaching Theme

Our texts from Isaiah 35 and Psalm 146 speak of the promised transformation of the reign of God. For Judean exiles mourning the traumatic loss of Jerusalem, the temple, and their own nationhood, hearing the promise of bountiful life for the desert, support for the weak, and healing for those with illnesses and disabilities represented profound good news. Old Testament professor Beth Tanner describes Psalm 146 as "an oasis."[8] I think the same metaphor could be used to describe Isaiah 35. After chapters of judgment, here is a word of hope.

Mary's song from Luke is an alternate text this week for the psalm reading. Like Isaiah and Psalm 146, Mary too sings of God's power to reverse the fortunes of the weak, hungry, and disadvantaged. Through the power of God, a young girl with little power will always be remembered for the way she assented to God. God has lifted her up to be used to bring Jesus into the world. While God lifts up those with no power, her song is a warning to those with power and privilege. God removes powerful leaders from their thrones and sends the rich away "empty-handed."

While it is tempting to read texts like these and see ourselves as the beneficiaries of God's promises, globally citizens of North America are often seen as rich and powerful. We use more than our share of the earth's resources and feel threatened by immigrants who seek safety. In what ways do these texts invite us to shrink our consumption and share our abundance so that others might have enough?

Responsive Prayer of Confession and Assurance

Scripture reminds us to wait patiently for the coming of the Lord,
But we grow weary. Weak and shaky, we lose resolve and complain.
Our hope dries up like temporary streams after a desert rain.
Our lives are thirsty for your presence!
Be strong! Don't fear! Our God is coming.
God is coming to save us.
Amidst the glory of the Lord, the desert will blossom.
The weak and sick will be healed.
God will bring justice for the oppressed, the hungry, the immigrants among us.
The dry and burning parts of our lives will burst forth with fountains and pools of water.
Grief and groaning will flee away.
The Lord will rule forever!

Benediction

May the spirit of God inspire you with patience and endurance in this season of longing and waiting. May you see signs of God's reign here and now. May God's refreshing promises create fountains of hope in the dry places of our lives so that we might share with others. The God who promises is faithful!

December 22, 2019–Fourth Sunday of Advent

Passages: Isaiah 7:10-16; Psalm 80:1-7, 17-19; Romans 1:1-7; Matthew 1:18-25

Preaching Theme

Suppose that one day you were reading a story in which an elderly woman is talking to her pregnant granddaughter. "Now listen, my dear," the old woman says, "I would ask that you name this child after your grandfather and so give him the name Nelson." Suppose the young woman agrees. "Okay, Grandma, his name will be Nelson." But then you read, "This fulfilled a prediction once made by the pregnant woman's father that her firstborn would be named 'Wallace.'" Well, which is it: Nelson or Wallace? So also in Matthew 1: the angel says to name the baby Jesus, and Matthew turns right around and says, "That's right: he's little baby Immanuel." And then the baby is born and he's "Jesus." Jesus. Immanuel. Immanuel. Jesus. Must we choose? No.

Apparently, you cannot speak the one without invoking the other. Jesus = Immanuel. Jesus = God with us. God with us in all our flesh-and-blood realities and messiness. God with us in diapers. God with us nursing at Mary's breast. God with us in learning to eat small pieces of bread and drinking from a cup without spilling milk all down his chin.

To riff on a well-known line from Teresa of Avila, we look for Christ among the pots and pans. Christ among the barn animals and then those quirky magi astrologers and then all the rest of the Gospel's curious cast of characters. God with us.

God with the prostitutes and the lepers and the outcast in whose company Jesus would delight again and again. God at the dinner table with a chive stuck between his incisors. God lifting the cup of wine to his lips. God with us.

God with the little children whose warm brows he touched and blessed. God smiling when a baby was shown to him by a proud new mother. God with us in all our ordinary times and days. God with us, as Jesus would say to bookend Matthew's Gospel, even unto the end of the ages. Always. With us. Immanuel.

Immanuel is God-with-us in the cancer clinic and at the local nursing home where bodies slump pitifully in wheelchairs pushed up against the hallway walls. Immanuel is God-with-us in the hospice room and when life's final breath slips past a dear one's teeth and lips. Immanuel is God-with-us when the pink slip comes and when the beloved child sneers, "I hate you!"

Immanuel is God-with-us when you pack the Christmas decorations away and, with an aching heart, realize afresh that your one son never did call over the holidays. Not once. Immanuel is God-with-us when your dear wife or mother stares at you with an Alzheimer's glaze and absently asks, "What was your name again, dear?" Ever and always Jesus stares straight into you with his two good eyes, and he does so not only when you can smile back but most certainly also when your own eyes are full of tears. In fact, Jesus is Immanuel, "God with you," even in those times when you are so angry with God that you refuse to meet his eyes. But even when you feel like you can't look at him, he never looks away from you. He can't.

His name says it all.

Secondary Preaching Theme

"To God's beloved ones in Rome." Such a commonplace way to open a letter. And it's easy to breeze right past it, hurry on by to get to the meat of the letter. But this time we cannot do that. Not with this salutation. Because it turns out that God has beloved children in Rome.

In Rome, you notice. The place, the time, make all the difference in the world. If you don't believe that, try on these acoustics: It is the darkest days of World War II. People are dying. Bombs are falling regularly from the skies. Jews have been rounded up, herded like cattle, and never seen again. Then: "To God's beloved ones in London." "To God's beloved ones in Berlin."

It is a time of state oppression of all things religious and holy. God has been declared dead, religion illegal or frowned upon. Then: To God's beloved ones in Moscow. To God's beloved ones in Wittenberg. To God's beloved ones in Beijing. To God's beloved ones in South Sudan and Darfur, to God's beloved ones in Aleppo and in Karachi, to God's beloved ones in southside Chicago and in Port-au-Prince, to God's beloved ones in Havana and in Pyongyang.

To God's beloved ones wherever God's people feel the love of God seems far away, wherever God's people feel exiled even if they are still living in the same place they've always been. To all God's beloved ones wherever they may be: grace to you, and, oh yes, also peace to you through God our Father and the Lord Jesus Christ.

That's no small thing to offer. In Advent and at all times, let's keep offering it to those who need it most.

Parting Words (from Psalm 80)

Revive us so that we can call on your name. Restore us, Lord God of heavenly forces! Make your face shine so that we can be saved!

December 25, 2019– Nativity of the Lord/ Christmas Day

Passages: Isaiah 9:2-7; Psalm 96; Titus 2:11-14; Luke 2:1-11, (15-20)

Call to Worship (from Psalm 96)

Sing to the Lord a new song! Sing to the Lord, all the earth!

Sing to the Lord! Bless his name! Share the news of his saving work every single day!

Declare God's glory among the nations; declare his wondrous works among all people,

Because the Lord is great and so worthy of praise. Joy to the world! The Savior has come!

Preaching Theme

Psychologists tell us that when we witness something of great moral beauty, we experience something called "elevation," which is the opposite of disgust or revulsion. We feel warm, encouraged, grateful when we encounter profound beauty and nobility. And I think this was the experience of the shepherds in Luke 2. They had witnessed something of profound moral beauty and had heard a message of radiant hope. And this elevation was even contagious. Luke tells us in verse 18 that everyone was amazed at "what the shepherds said."

But have you ever wondered just what it was they said? We're not told. But I suspect the best thing they took away from the whole encounter with the Christ child was something the angels said to them even before they had left for the stable. As older translations rendered it, "There is born *to you* this day in the city of David, a Savior." To you. This is your Savior.

What a wonderful, elevating message! This is not somebody else's story. This is the shepherds' own story. They are characters in the drama. The Savior was born for them, to them. That these musty, smelly, dirty shepherds got to meet this Savior in a barn merely confirmed it: this was indeed a Savior that fit normal folks like them.

Had they tried to visit the gilded crib of the Caesar's newborn son in some Roman palace, you get the feeling these fellows would not have gotten anywhere near the royal heir. Leastwise not without a serious bath and some new clothing! But the real Savior fit them. He was for them.

It's the same message every Christmas. Preachers get to declare to all kinds of people that on this day long ago a Savior had been born and he is for you. This was a truly elevating message for the shepherds when they encountered their very own Savior in that manger. It is most certainly not less so for us. If we can hear and believe that part of what the shepherds said, then no matter what happens once Christmas is past, we will be able to join those shepherds in glorifying and praising God for all that we have seen and heard. In the light of that, merely to say "Merry Christmas" seems weak.

Let's try instead a "Hallelujah!" For there has been born to you and for you a Savior. For you. For *you*.

Secondary Preaching Theme

Brave is the preacher who dares stray from Luke 2 on Christmas Day. And yet the epistle lesson from Titus 2 fits Christmas well and gives us a message we need at Christmas and beyond. The text is all about the "appearing" or the epiphany of the light of Christ in this world, including on the island of Crete where Titus ministered. Reading between the lines of Paul's letter, we discern Crete was a tough row to hoe. The residents there were notoriously lazy, self-indulgent, gluttonous, and cruel. They lived by their bellies more than their wits with an attitude of "If it feels good, do it." And they did.

The Greek word Paul uses for "self-control" all throughout his letter to Titus is *sophroneo*, which is a curious little word that literally means "to be in your right mind." The opposite of self-control, then, is to be out of your head or, as my mother used to put it when my brother and I did something particularly stupid, "Are you out of your ever-loving minds!!??" Doing whatever feels good is a crazy way to live because it means you are cut off from sensible, normal, creational limits—the stuff God put into place to protect us and to ensure our flourishing.

But not so for those who follow the child of Bethlehem whose appearing, Paul writes, teaches us to say no to such living. By the Spirit's power active in us, we can say no to bad things so we can be level-headed, self-controlled, and in our right minds.

It's not enough to celebrate Christ's birth once a year but then walk away from the manger unchanged. We have a whole, great big, beautiful gospel story to tell to the nations, and we tell it best when we live reasonable lives of self-control and love for others.

Despite what some people say, we really cannot "make Christmas last all year long." Who would want to? But we can make Christ and his appearing last all year long. We must. The grace of God has appeared to help us say no to all ungodliness and wild living so we can witness all the time to the one who we really do know is "the reason for the season."

December 29, 2019

Passages: Isaiah 63:7-9; Psalm 148; Hebrews 2:10-18; Matthew 2:13-23

Call to Worship (from Psalm 8)

Lord, our Lord,
How majestic is your name throughout the earth!
You made your glory higher than the heavens!
From the mouths of all people you have ordained praise.
Let us worship the Lord our God.
Hallelujah! Amen!

Preaching Theme

Wasn't it just Christmas four days ago? And now we have to read this story in Matthew 2? Matthew 1 told us that this little one would be Immanuel, God with us. But God no sooner arrives "with us" and the worlds of many families get turned upside down through the tragic, brutal murder of toddlers and infants.

It was Herod who went crazy, and that stands to reason as Herod was insane. To put it mildly, the magi had set a spark to a very bad powder keg. "You'd be better off as one of Herod's pigs than as one of his sons" the Caesar himself is said to have once remarked after hearing Herod had killed yet another son who seemed too eager to take Dad's place on the throne.

A "king of the Jews" was out there somewhere, the astrologers from Baghdad told Herod. This no doubt led Herod to punch a few holes in the palace walls after which he kicked the cat clear across a room. But then Herod managed to smooth back his hair, wipe the furious sweat off his brow, straighten up his royal robes, and reappear before the magi with the hollow words, "Well, good luck to you, gentlemen, and once you find the king you're looking for... um, er, let me know where he is. I have a little something for him myself. Can't wait to *give* it to the little fellow..."

God was several moves ahead of Herod, and so the magi are tipped off to scurry back to Baghdad by another way. Once Herod figures out he'd been out-foxed, he kicks a few more walls and throws another hissy fit before issuing a dark decree: kill all the babies in this area of a certain age and with luck, we'll take out this wannabe king while we're at it.

"The first martyrs," they have been called. The title doesn't really fit since a martyr is literally a "witness" who dies on account of not recanting his or her witness to the reality of Jesus as God and Lord. The babies in question—and their parents for that matter—had in fact never heard of Jesus, had no faith to profess or recant. All they could do is suffer a cruel fate for reasons many of those parents may never have come remotely close to figuring out.

Why must the world react to the advent of the Christ with violence? Then again, why not? Let's admit that this is a horrible story. But let's acknowledge that every day the news is filled with the same thing. It's a brutal world God came to save. God knew it would not be easy. Not by a long shot. God knew that it would never work to wait for his creatures to get their acts together and meet him halfway, or a quarter of the way, or a tenth of the way. God was going to have to do this bloody work himself, and the slaughter of the innocents is proof positive of both the long odds God faced and at the same time the very reason the work had to be done by God's Son in the first place.

Secondary Preaching Theme

God's power cannot cut it. That's the bottom line of Hebrews 2. Isn't that counterintuitive? People who run for high office are sometimes accused of being overly ambitious, of being "power crazy" and unduly hungry for authority. And at times these people are that, but just as often it is the case that if you genuinely want to make a difference for the country, the state, the county, the city, you need to get elected to do it because only then are you in a position to help the most people the most effectively. You need power to get things done in this world. That's simply how it goes.

But the great irony and paradox of the gospel is that although no one had a bigger set of problems to solve than God did in considering how best to save this cosmos, at the end of the day God concluded that his omnipotent power alone was not enough to seal the deal. Yes, the author to the Hebrews muses, maybe power would have been enough to save angels or something, but it would not be enough to save flesh-and-blood human beings. No, these folks will need to be saved by another way and in the great reversal of all our normal thinking on such matters, the way forward for that salvation was going to lead smack through the way of weakness.

God was going to need some power, yes, it's true. But the greatest display of that power would come when he had to raise a limp, dead-as-a-doornail human person from the grave. Up until then it was the frailty of a real human life that would be the epicenter of all things salvific. A few days after Christmas, that is a mystery well worth pondering.

Excerpt from *How to Preach a Dangerous Sermon* by Frank Thomas

Editor's Note: In his book How to Preach a Dangerous Sermon, *Frank A. Thomas suggests that we are in a cultural moment when we need dangerous preaching, prophetic preaching, preaching to unmask the illusions of our age and the tyranny of ideologies that are the opposite of Christ's gospel and of the message of God's love for all, starting with those who are poor and disenfranchised. In this excerpt Thomas makes a case for a gospel-infused moral imagination in preaching by highlighting the moral imagination of contemporary America and the ways this American imagination is the counterpoint to a true moral imagination rooted in Christ.*

The moral imagination of America is dominated primarily by the idolatrous and diabolical imagination. American moral imagination will always eventually slide to the idolatrous and diabolical imagination as long as ritual of benefit and freedom are the domain of a few. I want the reader to clearly understand the reasoning behind my judgment that America's moral imagination is dominated by the idolatrous and diabolical imagination by looking at four critical ideas: (1) a balanced view of the American character and identity, (2) the rituals and benefits of freedom for a few, (3) the quest to perfect our Union, and (4) white supremacy and the refusal of equality.

First, it is critically important in discerning the moral imagination of America that we take a balanced view of American cultural identity, and therefore the char-acter of America. The fundamental cultural myth of America is a city set on a hill, blessed by God to be the light of the world, with the spiritual values of optimism, hard work, frugality, capitalistic economic striving, and a virgin land as assets to bring the kingdom of God to earth.[1] This cultural myth formed a "centrality" that bound the American nation together in common habits, language, beliefs, and values. Even as cultural myth binds a people together, it also limits their perspective, and in some sense blinds them. The blindness in regard to the cultural myth of America is found by asking who in the society is excluded, marginalized, subjugated, domesticated, and in some cases, even defined as less than human. How does the cultural myth of America function in regard to the respect and treatment of indigenous cultures and people, including groups denied freedom, equality, citizenship, economic participa-tion, voting rights, and so on, in other words, the domination of subjected people?

Scavan Bercovitch, the Canadian literary and cultural critic, who was a leader and influential figure in the field of American Studies, presents a true and balanced view of American character and cultural identity. Bercovitch comments on the twin dynamics of empire, the creative energy and the violence of America:

> As I followed its (American cultural myth) changing terms of identity (Puritan errand, national mission, Manifest Destiny, the dream) the windings of language turned out to be matters of history. "America" as an act of symbolic appropriation came alive to me as the twin dynamics of empire: on one hand, a process of violence unparalleled (proportionately) by even the Spanish conquistadors and sustained in the twentieth century by a rhetoric of holy war against everything un-American; on the other hand, an unleashing of creative energies—enterprise, speculation, community building, personal initiative, industry, confidence, idealism, and hope—unsurpassed by any other modern nation. What I discovered in the interconnections between violence and culture formation was transcendence in action: "America," an interpretation, through which the worlds out there had been triumphantly repressed, rhetorically and historically—first, by the myths of their inhabitants ("savage," "primitive") attended by the facts of genocide and then by symbols of the land ("virgin," "wilderness") attended by the creation of the United States as "America."[2]

Just as it is difficult for an individual to have an honest and balanced view of themselves, given the complexity of motives, drives, rationalizations, self-interest, and morals in any action or decision, it is very difficult for most Americans to take a balanced view of America. Most tend to view America from the perspective of patriotism and laud the greatness of America, or, on the other hand, with a view to conquest and oppression, and therefore extol the violence and cruelty of America. When we look at the total picture of American character, America has both released more creative energy into the world than any modern nation in history, and yet, has also been imperialistic and violent on an unparalleled level. Often, America celebrates the industry, confidence, idealism, and hope of America, yet ignores the effects of imperialism, violence, discrimination, racism, slavery, misogyny, genocide, and the conquest of indigenous people. Americans have a very difficult time coming to terms with the twin dynamics of empire, often residing in the concept of American exceptionalism and leading to American imperialism. Without a balanced view of American greatness and American violence, we can never accurately ascertain the true moral imagination of America.

The second aspect of discerning the moral imagination of America is to accept and come to terms with the truth that the ritual and benefit of freedom of America has *always* been restricted to a few certain privileged groups within American culture. In examining the plight of mid-nineteenth-century feminists as one of those excluded from freedom, Bercovitch points out:

> When William Arthur spoke of "the American," he was not thinking of people like Margaret Fuller—or for that matter, of Fredrick Douglass, Black Hawk, Rabbi Isaac Meyer Wise, of John England, the Catholic Bishop of South Carolina...[3]

Jeremiah

The truth is historically, and even at that this present moment, there have been and are people marginalized and excluded from being "Americans." While we must acknowledge that progress has been made, we must also acknowledge that freedom has been painfully slow. American rituals and benefits of freedom have been intended for a few because certain groups were and are considered less than "Americans" and "other." Hence the oppressive and dismissive language of "take our country back," and defining certain groups as "real Americans."

Michael Novak argues that the "adolescent American dream is ethnocentric," that is, "its primary symbols are white Anglo American, Protestant, and male."[4] In accordance with American exceptionalism, Novak concludes that "the central axis of world history, according to this [American] dream, pivots on the history of the Anglo-American race."[5] Notice Novak's use of the word "adolescent," meaning that the American Dream can mature to include, based upon protest and dissent across time, some of the very people who were once excluded, and often has, more prominently with European immigrants than with anyone else. This brings us to the third factor in discerning the moral imagination of America, perfecting the Union.

In my book, *American Dream 2.0: A Christian Way Out of the Great Recession*, I detail the media firestorm of March 13, 2008, and beyond created by the airing of sound bites of the sermons of Jeremiah Wright Jr.[6] For many, Wright's comments had the potential to decimate the presidential hopes of then-candidate Barack Obama. Obama was forced to deliver a speech entitled, "A More Perfect Union," on March 18, in Philadelphia, Pennsylvania. Reminiscent of John F. Kennedy's 1960 presidential campaign speech before Protestant leaders to address the issue of his Roman Catholic faith and the separation of church and state, Obama's address was highly anticipated and certain to be highly scrutinized. The issue for Obama was squarely race, with all of the tension and anxiety that race in America engenders.

In this speech, Obama gave a balanced view of both the greatness of America, including the idea of democracy in the Declaration of Independence and Constitution, and American racism, imperialism, and genocide. The flaw in the document, or "stain" as Obama suggests, was the "nation's original sin of slavery." Slavery divided the colonies and the 1787 Philadelphia convention until it was agreed to allow the slave trade to continue for at least twenty more years, leaving "any final resolution to future generations." The bedrock theme of Obama's speech is his conviction of the responsibility of each succeeding generation to perfect the Union started by the founding fathers. Obama resolves the twin dynamics of American empire by shifting from a focus on past and traditional greatness (the subtext of which includes racism, of course) to the perfection and completion of America's greatness at some point in the future by succeeding generations. Each generation must do its part, but the fulfillment of the ideals will only happen in the future. The source of Obama's thought about perfecting the Union is Abraham Lincoln, who championed the perfection of the nation's core ideals to be realized at some future point.

In a series of debates with Stephen Douglass in 1858, Lincoln argued that the Declaration of Independence is not a static document with fixed truths completed in the past, but rather presented Americans with ideals as maxims, goals to be strived for that guide thought and action. Douglass argued against the equality of all human beings and contended that the Declaration of Independence did not apply to blacks. In the final debate in Alton, Illinois, Lincoln refuted this claim by making equality a maxim rather than a fixed truth.[7] For Lincoln, the Declaration of Independence sets forth general truths, rules of conduct, or fundamental principles such as equality, that only could be perfected at some point in the future. Obama followed Lincoln's strategy and attempted to bridge America's racial divide.

Obama admits that the ideal of American democracy is great and remarkable and the implementation of the founding ideal of America was flawed. Obama resolves this tension by suggesting that the design of America is to perfect the Union in succeeding generations. Obama attempts to change the fixed narrative of racial discourse in America by suggesting that it is the responsibility of white and blacks to perfect the Union rather than to focus exclusively on white or black grievances and trauma. This leads to the final idea to discuss in this Introduction: White supremacy and refusal of the challenges of equality.

White supremacy refuses to accept the challenge of equality, and thus refuses to perfect the Union. I use the phrase white supremacy, even though it can be incendiary, so let me briefly explain what I mean.

In the upcoming Chapter One entitled, "Race, Shrinking Whiteness: Four Qualities of the Moral Imagination of Robert F. Kennedy," following Thomas Kane, I give a fuller explanation and discussion of my definition of white supremacy. Most Americans have a narrow and limited view of white supremacy. For them, white supremacy is reduced to individuals saying the n-word, individuals committing acts of violence physically or psychologically against persons of color, or historical attitudes and passions that have long passed, such as slavery, lynching, and the signs of a white and colored segregated Jim Crow America. With this narrow definition, it would appear to many that white supremacy is gone. Quite to the contrary, the conscious and unconscious acts, and the intentions of white supremacy are well and alive. They are covertly institutionalized, such as in systems of mass incarceration, police shooting and killing unarmed African American people, tactics of voter suppression, and the race-baiting and hatred of Alt-Rights groups, to name a few. These institutionalized racial systems and people in the systems believe and ensure that the majority of material goods, services, and resources be reserved for persons of European descent.

For generations, many white Americans have chosen and continue to choose the comfort of apathy regarding resource inequity over the genuine challenge of equality—material, political, rhetorical, and representational. The source of this denial of equality is hotly debated and attributed as racial hostility by some and racial indifference by others. Michele Alexander defines racial indifference as "a lack of compassion and caring about race and racial groups," and defines racial hostility as the assumption that systems are "necessarily predicated on the desire to harm other racial groups."[8] Alexander posits racial indifference and the "comfort of apathy" as overarching sources of the refusal of the vast majority of white Americans to take up the challenge of equality—material, political, rhetorical, and representational. The late Derrick Bell of New York University Law School, one of the founders of Critical Race Theory and the concept of "interest convergence," made the argument that whites will not support civil rights policies that may threaten white social status. He maintained that from the beginning of America, the framers of the Constitution chose the "original sin," rewards of property over justice. Bell believed that white people would support racial justice when there is something in it for them, when there is a convergence between the interests of white people and racial justice. Bell asserted that the Supreme Court ended the longstanding policy in 1954 of "separate but equal" in *Brown v. Board of Education* as a result of the embarrassment of segregation before the world, hence the need to support civil and human rights, given the Cold War with the Soviet Union.[9] Whether the source is racial indifference, racial hostility, or a lack of interest convergence, the bottom line is white supremacy authorizes white privilege and refuses the challenge of equality in America.

The sum total of a balanced view of the American character and identity, the rituals and benefits of freedom for a few, the quest to perfect our Union, and the white supremacy refusal of equality is that the moral imagination of America in the second decade of the twenty-first century is dominated by the idolatrous and diabolical imagination. Again, what has and always will hinder the moral imagination of America is white supremacy that reserves the rights and benefits of America only to a few. The election of Donald Trump—who trumpets cynicism, white nationalism, patriarchy, ridicule of immigrants and women and disabled persons, a Muslim ban, and the support of Trump from the KKK and Alt-Rights racist groups—is indicative of the pervasiveness of the idolatrous and diabolical imagination. Let me be crystal clear: racism, misogyny, cynicism, xenophobia, patriarchy, and anti-immigrant blame discourse always surges from the heart of the diabolical imagination.

Excerpt from *Exodus Preaching: Crafting Sermons about Justice and Hope* by Kenyatta Gilbert

Editor's Note: In his book Exodus Preaching: Crafting Sermons about Justice and Hope, *Kenyatta R. Gilbert contends that in difficult times such as we have been experiencing in recent years, the heart of African American prophetic preaching—Exodus preaching—helps us reclaim our hope as believers in Christ. He also believes that there are a bevy of preachers today—many still quite young—who are carrying out this kind of preaching. In this book Gilbert repeatedly gives readers a welter of practical tips for crafting this kind of Exodus preaching and he further illustrates all those techniques with extensive excerpts from many of today's finest preachers. In this excerpt Gilbert sketches the broader landscape of our world and how Exodus preaching can engage this world.*

Times are dark. But hope remains in reach. Among the many words that leave the preacher's lips, no Christian preacher escapes the obligation to set this declaration before the people. Why? Because preaching is what *hope* looks like in our age of compassion fatigue, conspicuous consumption, and deadly violence. Though not an end in itself, preaching is a means by which God reminds a society of God's concern for community wellness, life, human dignity, and freedom in a less-than-perfect world. This is why preaching and preachers matter.

What Is Exodus Preaching?

African American prophetic preaching (alternatively termed *Exodus preaching*) is "interpretation" that brings clarity to the sacred (the realities of God, revealed truth, highest moral values, and so on) and articulates what should be appropriate human response to the sacred. The preacher who preaches prophetically does not treat social justice (or other sacred values) as something independent from God but as being rooted in and emanating from God. *Exodus preaching* does not take place in a vacuum, nor is it self-generated discourse; rather, it is daring speech that offers a vision of divine intent. It reveals a picture of what God intends and expects of God's human creation—a picture that enables persons and faith communities to interpret their situation in light of God's justice, and to name as sin activities that frustrate God's life-giving purposes.

African American prophetic preaching is meditational speech. It bears no fundamental distinction from prophetic preaching in general, except to the extent that it is seen as God-summoned speech clothed in cultural particularity.[1] Contextual awareness in preaching helps us to see that we bring ourselves to the scriptural texts we interpret, and our seeing, if we see anything at all, is revealed through the lens of our lived experience. Regarding context and culture, one must keep in mind that Jesus of Nazareth was not a rich Palestinian Jew—a revolutionary figure nonetheless—who lived more than two thousand years ago in a living community. In other words, Jesus had a specific ethnic and religious identity, and this is not insignificant given Western culture's enduring fascination and general depiction of Jesus as a Nordic martyr. A Jesus separated from his Judaic heritage and social location renders Jesus ahistorical, mythical, and incapable of saving humanity.

Because human beings are literally thrown into traditions and communities from which they take their personhood and socializations, racially and ethnically blind preaching can only exist in the colonized mind. This is fact, not fiction. As God-summoned proclamation that lifts and values the reality that sociocultural context shapes preachers and their sermons, *Exodus preaching* sees the homiletical life through the religious practices and lived experiences of Gentile Christians of African descent in North America and is written from this perspective....

Exodus preaching (African American prophetic preaching) is concrete and daring discourse that names God and offers a vision of divine purpose. Preaching of this kind serves an emancipatory agenda. Through criticism and symbols of hope about what God intends and expects of God's human creation, Exodus preaching lands on the ear of the despairing and dedicated to help them interpret their situation in light of God's justice and the quest for human freedom. As long as people desire to be free, Martin King's insightful query will never ring hollow.

King once asked, "Who is it that is supposed to articulate the longings of people more than the preacher?" Such a question hoists a burden upon every minister who hopes to do something of consequence in partnership with God. To shun the beckoning task of preparing listeners to stand and be counted as co-participants with a promise-bearing God at work in the world is to tighten Egypt's grip and undermine a several-centuries-old quest for freedom. The Exodus saga's correspondence with today's victims of history has added legitimacy to the preacher's speech about God's will toward justice. Likewise, the Hebrew prophet's evocative cries for moral accountability to God and community beckons preachers toward high standards of moral and ethical responsibility, just as the salvific agenda and incarnational witness of Jesus remind preachers that the vocation of prophetic truth-telling often co-occurs with personal suffering. Such orienting biblical touchstones invite today's preacher-prophets to stand against the forces of death and evil in both the public square and the church. This is why the enduring pursuit for human dignity and overcoming spiritual and social forces that work against the collective good and welfare of all persons remain so important. In today's culture of trauma and numbness, if the preacher is silent potential pathways to human flourishing will be blocked.

But what might these pathways resemble? I have argued elsewhere that prophetic proclamation is not self-generated discourse but summoned Word taking its beginning and ending in God.[2] Yet because preaching is both a divine and human activity, which calls upon a preacher's gifts and faculties, I believe that strategies to push a preacher to stretch her theological imagination can aid the preacher's growth, especially as it relates to developing a prophetic consciousness given the current state of the world.

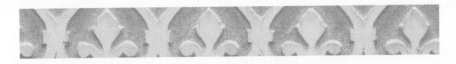

Excerpt from *The End of Preaching* by Tom Troeger

Editor's Note: In his book The End of Preaching, *Thomas Troeger asks the funda-mental question, "What is the end of preaching?" Why do we preach? What should it accomplish? Answers to this question across church history have been legion but Troeger believes that an excellent answer to the question is that the end of preaching is prayer. The purpose and conclusion of preaching should be to create in the listeners a relationship with God characterized by fervent prayer that, in turn, captures the whole sweep of the Chris-tian life from adoration to confession, from thanks to petition, from praise to doxology. If preaching creates a praying people who have the kind of close relationship with God that a vigorous prayer life needs in order to be sustained, then the word of God will have taken deep root indeed on account of the word preached. In this excerpt, Troeger explains his definition of the end of preaching being prayer.*

To say that "preaching's the end of prayer" is to affirm that one of the tasks of preaching is to awaken us to the realization that we walk every day in the weather of prayer. But how is preaching to accomplish this when prayer is itself such a sprawling, varied, multidimensional, primordial reality?

George Herbert provides us with a framework for responding to this question through his metaphor of the temple. Carol and Philip Zaleski reflect on how temples help to sustain the praying that goes on in a multitude of places: "We may pray in the bedroom at dawn, in the fields at midday, in the kitchen at dusk. But we are able to pray there because we pray also in a more powerful place, where prayer goes on endlessly, day and night. Prayer does have a wellspring, and its name is the temple."[1]

When Herbert says "praying's the end of preaching," he has in mind the prayer of the temple, the prayer of the house of worship, the prayer of the church gathered together in holy service. For Herbert the corporate nature of prayer does not domes-ticate and smooth the ragged edges of what the human heart wants from God. Mark the astounding range of images and phrases that Herbert employs in this sonnet that is one continuous series of appositions for prayer:

> Prayer the Church's banquet, angel's age,
>   God's breath in man returning to his birth,
>   The soul in paraphrase, heart in pilgrimage,
> The Christian plummet sounding heav'n and earth
> Engine against th' Almighty, sinner's tow'r,
>   Reversed thunder, Christ-side-piercing spear,
>   The six-days world transposing in an hour,

A kind of tune, which all things hear and fear;
Softness, and peace, and joy, and love, and bliss,
    Exalted manna, gladness of the best,
    Heaven in ordinary, man well drest,
The milky way, the bird of Paradise,
    Church-bells beyond the stars heard, the soul's blood,
    The land of spices; something understood.[2]

The title of each chapter in this book is drawn directly from Herbert's sonnet. This chapter is entitled, "The Church's Banquet," the opening phrase the poet uses to describe prayer in his sonnet. If prayer is "the Church's banquet," and if we claim that "praying's the end of preaching," then that means the purpose of preaching is to invite people to a banquet, a feast, a celebratory meal.

Although Herbert's focus is on corporate prayer, he does appreciate the importance of private personal prayer. Early in "The Church-Porch" he counsels the following:

By all means use sometimes to be alone.
Salute thyself: see what thy soul doth wear.
Dare to look in thy chest; for 'tis thine own:
And tumble up and down what thou find'st there.[3]

Some forty stanzas later, however, shortly before Herbert asserts that "praying's the end of preaching" he observes the following:

Though private prayer be a brave design,
Yet public hath more promises, more love:
And love's a weight to hearts, to eyes a sign.
We all are but cold suitors; let us move
    Where it is warmest. Leave thy six and seven;
    Pray with the most: for where most pray, is heaven.[4]

Thus, when Herbert says "praying's the end of preaching," he means the corporate prayer of the community of faith: "the Church's banquet."

I believe the poet's counsel about the prayer of the community would strengthen a lot of the preaching. With notable exceptions, the majority of preaching I have heard over the last forty-six years focused more on the individual than the gathered body of Christ. Herbert calls us out of our isolation to join with one another:

We all are but cold suitors; let us move
    Where it is warmest. Leave thy six and seven;
    Pray with the most: for where most pray, is heaven.[5]

Although the "public" prayer of our houses of worship is highly varied, it tends to fall into recognizable patterns that reach across many traditions, no matter how much the style and form of their services may differ. I am thinking of six classic kinds of corporate prayer, each of them expressing a different dimension in the divine/human relationship and each of them manifest in one way or another in a wide range of worship practices:

Adoration
Confession
Supplication
Intercession
Thanksgiving
Lament

To say "praying's the end of preaching" is to say adoration is the end of preaching. Confession is the end of preaching. Supplication is the end of preaching. Intercession is the end of preaching. Thanksgiving is the end of preaching. Lament is the end of preaching. In drawing this implication from Herbert's assertion, I am not claiming that this was the poet's intention. Rather I am using Herbert's poetry to fuel my own work of imaginative homiletical theology.

The six categories of prayer I have named obviously do not exhaust all the forms that prayer may take, but they are comprehensive enough to provide insight into the sprawling, complex, multidimensional, primordial phenomenon of prayer. I will use these six forms of prayer to symbolize and explore the virtually unlimited repertoire of prayer. My aim is to illuminate the theological implications and homiletical possibilities that open up when "praying's the end of preaching."

Since prayer, whatever form it takes, cultivates a living relationship to God, Herbert's statement means that the end of preaching is the vitalizing, nurturing, enriching, deepening, broadening, heightening of our relationship to God.

If the end of preaching is prayer, the richness of prayer, the fullness of prayer, the complexity of prayer, the multidimensionality of prayer, the primordial character of prayer, then a question every preacher and every listener to sermons needs to ask is: what kind of prayer is awakened by the sermons I preach or hear?

I am *not* saying every sermon ought to be about prayer nor that every sermon will conclude with the preacher offering a prayer. Rather I am asking what kind of living relationship to God does preaching nurture over time? Is it only the relationship of the individual to God? Or does our preaching strengthen the communal relationship between God and the gathered people of God? Does it welcome people to "the Church's banquet?"

Notes

Editor's Introduction

1. The Beatles, vocal performance of "With a Little Help from My Friends," by John Lennon and Paul McCartney, recorded March 29–30, 1967, on *Sgt. Pepper's Lonely Hearts Club Band*, Parlophone PMC 7027.

January

1. "James Cameron Ventures to Ocean's Deepest Point," CBC News, March 25, 2012, http://www.cbc.ca/news/world/james-cameron-ventures-to-ocean-s-deepest-point-1.1151694.

February

1. James H. Cone, *A Black Theology of Liberation* (Maryknoll, NY: Orbis Press, 1996), 3.

2. Assata Shakur, *Assata: An Autobiography* (Chicago: Lawrence Hill Books, 2001), 154.

March

1. Quoted from a Churchill speech in William Safire, *Safire's Political Dictionary*, 5th ed. (Oxford: Oxford University Press, 2008), 474.

April

1. John Wesley, *Hymns and Sacred Poems* (1739; Ann Arbor, MI: University of Michigan Library, 2007), viii.

2. Mark A. Matson, *John*, Interpretation Bible Studies (Louisville: Westminster John Knox, 2002), unit 7, ebook edition.

3. Beverly Roberts Gaventa, *The New Interpreter's Bible One-Volume Commentary* (Nashville: Abingdon Press, 2010), ebook edition.

4. Mark A. Matson, *John*, Interpretation Bible Studies (Louisville: Westminster John Knox, 2002), unit 7, ebook edition.

May

1. Mother Teresa, *In the Heart of the World: Thoughts, Stories, and Prayers* (Novato, CA: New World Library, 1997), 23.

2. Augustine, quoted in Pierre Pourrat, *Christian Spirituality in the Middle Ages* (Pine Beach, NJ: The Newman Press, 1953), 291.

June

1. John Calvin, *Institutes of the Christian Religion*, trans. Ford Lewis Battles, ed. John T. McNeill, vol. 1 (Philadelphia: The Westminster Press, 1960), 523.

2. Douglas Farrow, *Ascension and Ecclesia: On the Significance of the Doctrine of the Ascension for Ecclesiology and Christian Cosmology* (Grand Rapids: William B. Eerdmans, 1999), 271n59.

3. Howard Thurman, *The Luminous Darkness: A Personal Interpretation of the Anatomy of Segregation and the Ground of Hope* (New York: Harper & Row, 1965).

July

1. James D. Bratt, ed., *Abraham Kuyper: A Centennial Reader* (Grand Rapids: Eerdmans, 1998), 488.

2. John Piper, *God Is the Gospel: Meditations on God's Love as the Gift of Himself* (Wheaton, IL: Crossway Books, 2005), 15 quoted in Francis Chan, *Crazy Love* (Colorado Springs, CO: David C. Cook Publishing, 2008), 100.

3. Issac Watts, "Joy to the World," *The United Methodist Hymnal* (Nashville: The United Methodist Publishing House, 1989), 246.

September

1. Dallas Willard, *The Divine Conspiracy: Rediscovering Our Hidden Life in God* (San Francisco: Harper, 1998).

2. Rachel Carson, *Silent Spring* (New York: Houghton Mifflin, 2002).

October

1. Sean Canino, "Photography's Contribution to the Civil Rights Movement," *Duke Today*, November 1, 2003, https://today.duke.edu/2003/11/raiford1118.html.

2. Joe Iovino, "All Saints Day: A Holy Day John Wesley Loved," UMC.org., October 28, 2015, http://www.umc.org/what-we-believe/all-saints-day-a-holy-day-john-wesley-loved.

November

1. Brenda B. Colijn, *Images of Salvation in the New Testament* (Downers Grove, IL: IVP, 2010), 162.

2. "They Paid for Wedding Dresses, Then the Company Went Out of Business," NPR Weekend Edition, radio transcript, July 16, 2017, http://www.npr .org/2017/07/16/537509436/they-paid-for-wedding-dresses-then-the-company -went-out-of-business.

December

1. "Live Like We're Dying," by Daniel John O'Donoghue, Andrew Frampton, Mark Anthony Sheehan, and Steve Kipner, vocal performance by Kris Allen, released September 21, 2009, on *Kris Allen*, Jive and 19 Recordings.

2. Marie Kondo, *The Life-Changing Magic of Tidying Up: The Japanese Art of Decluttering and Organizing* (Berkley, CA: Ten Speed Press, 2014).

3. O. Wesley Allen Jr., *Matthew* (Minneapolis: Fortress Press, 2013), 34–35.

4. Ibid., 35.

5. "About," Dallas Street Choir, accessed November 3, 2017, https://www .dallasstreetchoir.org/about-2/.

6. Allen, *Matthew*, 125.

7. Mother Teresa, *Mother Teresa: Come Be My Light: The Private Writings of the Saint of Calcutta*, ed. Brian Kolodiejchuk (New York: Doubleday Religion, 2007).

8. Beth L. Tanner, "Commentary on Psalm 146," Working Preacher, accessed November 3, 2017, http://www.workingpreacher.org/preaching .aspx?commentary_id=2676.

Excerpt from *How to Preach a Dangerous Sermon* by Frank Thomas

1. For a deeper treatment of "a city set on a hill," please see Frank A. Thomas, *American Dream 2.0: A Christian Way Out of the Great Recession*, "Section One: The Rise and Fall of the American Dream" (Nashville: Abingdon Press, 2012), 1–27.

2. Sacvan Bercovitch, *The American Jeremiad* (Madison: University of Wisconsin Press, 1978), 978–79.

3. Sacvan Bercovitch, "Investigations of an Americanist," in *The Journal of American History*, vol. 78, no. 3 (Dec 1991), 160.

4. Michael Novak, *Choosing Our King: Powerful Symbols in Presidential Politics* (New York: McMillan, 1974), 290.

5. Ibid.

6. Thomas, *American Dream 2.0: A Christian Way.*

7. Lincoln-Douglass Debate, Last Joint Debate at Alton, Illinois, October 15, 1858, http://www.bartleby.com/251/72.html (accessed 3/17/17).

8. Michele Alexander, *The New Jim Crow: Mass Incarceration in the Age of Colorblindness* (New York: The New Press, 2010), 203.

9. Bell is the source of Barak Obama's aforementioned use of racism as America's "original sin." The best source for an overall perspective of Bell's writings is *The Derrick Bell Reader*, eds., Richard Delegado, Jean Stefanic (New York: New York University Press, 2005).

Excerpt from *Exodus Preaching* by Kenyatta Gilbert

1. Kenyatta R. Gilbert, *A Pursued Justice: Black Preaching from the Great Migration to Civil Rights* (Waco, TX: Baylor University Press, 2016), 6.

2. Ibid.

Excerpt from *The End of Preaching* by Tom Troeger

1. Philip Zaleski and Carol Zaleski, *Prayer: A History* (Boston: Houghton Mifflin Company, 2005), 241.

2. George Herbert, "Prayer (I)," https://www.poetryfoundation.org/poems/44371/prayer-i. Public domain.

3. George Herbert, "Perirrhanterium," stanza 25. Public domain.

4. Ibid., stanza 67. Public domain. *Six and seven* is originally a dicing term that came to mean "indifference to the consequence of your action." George Herbert, *The Complete English Poems*, ed. John Tobin (London: Penguin Books, 1991), 330.

5. George Herbert, "Perirrhanterium," stanza 67. Public domain.

Contributors: Lectionary Sermon and Worship Helps

Josh Davis—Multiethnic Worship Leader, Founder, Proskuneo, Clarkson, GA
April 19, 2019; April 21, 2019; April 28, 2019; May 5, 2019

Yvette Davis—Pastor, Grace United Methodist Church, Harrisburg, PA
August 4, 2019; August 11, 2019; August 18, 2019; August 25, 2019

DJ Del Rosario—
March 31, 2019; April 7, 2019; April 14, 2019; April 18, 2019

Magrey DeVega—Pastor, Hyde Park United Methodist Church, Tampa, FL
March 3, 2019; March 10, 2019; March 17, 2019; March 24, 2019

Elisabeth DeVries—Graduate Student in Homiletics, Emmanuel College, Toronto, Ontario, Canada
June 9, 2019; June 16, 2019; June 23, 2019; June 30, 2019

Chelsey Harmon—Pastor, Christ Community Church, Nanaimo, BC, Canada
January 6, 2019; January 13, 2019; January 20, 2019; January 27, 2019

Scott Hoezee, General Editor—Director, The Center for Excellence in Preaching, Calvin Theological Seminary, Grand Rapids, MI
September 1, 2019; September 8, 2019; September 15, 2019; September 22, 2019; December 22, 2019; December 25, 2019; December 29, 2019

Juan Huertas—Pastor, Grace Community United Methodist Church, Shreveport, LA
September 29, 2019; October 6, 2019; October 13, 2019; October 20, 2019

Meg Jenista—Pastor, The Washington DC Christian Reformed Church, Washington, DC
July 7, 2019; July 14, 2019; July 21, 2019; July 28, 2019

F. Willis Johnson Jr.—Pastor, Wellspring Church, Ferguson, MO
February 3, 2019; February 10, 2019; February 17, 2019; February 24, 2019

Joseph D. Kim—Associate Pastor, Bothell United Methodist Church, Bothell, WA
October 27, 2019; November 3, 2019; November 10, 2019; November 17, 2019

Joni Sancken—Associate Professor of Homiletics, United Theological Seminary, Dayton, OH
November 24, 2019; December 1, 2019; December 8, 2019; December 15, 2019

Laura Truax—Pastor, LaSalle Street Church, Chicago, IL
May 12, 2019; May 19, 2019; May 26, 2019; June 2, 2019

Contributors: Full Sermon Texts

O. Wesley Allen Jr.—Professor of Homiletics, Southern Methodist University, Dallas, TX
"Praying In-Between" (Luke 18:1-8)

Scott Hoezee, General Editor—Director, The Center for Excellence in Preaching, Calvin Theological Seminary, Grand Rapids, MI
"Christ the Hen" (Luke 13:31-35)

Karoline M. Lewis—Associate Professor of Biblical Preaching, Luther Seminary, Saint Paul, MN
"On Being Jesus's Mother" (John 2:1-11)

Lia McIntosh—Associate Director, Center for Congregational Excellence, and Mission, Service, and Justice Ministries, Missouri Conference of The United Methodist Church
"Crazy Love: The Search for the Unquenchable" (Luke 10:38-42)

Ted A. Smith—Associate Professor of Preaching and Ethics, Candler School of Theology, Atlanta, GA
"After Ascension, Church" (Acts 1:1-14)

Subject Index

Scripture Index